THE MAN WHO STAYED AFLOAT

CAPTAIN JOHN'S CANADIAN JOURNEY

Fraser Sutherland

BookLand press

Published by BookLand Press
15 Allstate Parkway, Suite 600, Markham, Ontario L3R 5B4
www.booklandpress.com

Printed and bound in Canada.

Front cover photos by Boris Spremo, C.M.
Author's back cover photo by Irene Li.

Library and Archives Canada Cataloguing in Publication

Sutherland, Fraser
The man who stayed afloat: Captain John's Canadian journey/Fraser Sutherland.

Also issued in electronic format.
ISBN 978-1-926956-16-9

1. Letnik, Ivan. 2. Restaurateurs--Canada--Biography. 3. Ship captains--Canada--Biography. 4. Slovenian Canadians--Canada--Biography. 5. Toronto (Ont.)--Biography. I. Title.

TX910.5.L48S88 2012 647.95092 C2012-902974-2

Canada Council for the Arts Conseil des arts du Canada
ONTARIO ARTS COUNCIL CONSEIL DES ARTS DE L'ONTARIO

We acknowledge the support of the Canada Council for the Arts, which last year invested $154 million to bring the arts to Canadians throughout the country. We acknowledge the support of the Ontario Arts Council (OAC), an agency of the Government of Ontario, which last year funded 1,681 individual artists and 1,125 organizations in 216 communities across Ontario for a total of $52.8 million. We acknowledge the financial support of the Ontario Media Development Corporation for our publishing activities.

TABLE OF CONTENTS

CRUNCH

It was June 2, 1981. At 9 p.m. the hours of sun were lengthening toward what would soon be the longest day of the year for Captain John, the dusk thinking about turning into night. The sky was cloudless and the temperature was pleasant. Passing through its brief spring interregnum, Toronto had not yet entered its summer phase. Overall it was a perfect clement night for dining in mildly exotic surroundings, at least as exotic as it got on the waterfront. Urban American tourists were sure that the waterfront, like the other neighbourhoods they frequented, was *safe*. The belief had some substance in reality: Torontonians were notably polite, and their city remarkably safe considering its size.

Strolling along, our timidly adventurous diners, having driven in from the outer reaches of boroughs like Etobicoke or North York, or just off a tour bus, saw a looming sign at Queen's Quay West that marked their dining destination. One of two destinations actually, because Captain John's Harbour Boat Restaurant provided its food and entertainment aboard a pair of vessels. The one nearest to hand, docked parallel to the street, was the squat white, *Normac,* red-trimmed and with a red-painted hull, a former Detroit fire tug, later a car ferry. In 1969, the eponymous Captain John had brought it back from a coma in the Lake Erie port of Wallaceburg. On its funnel was the legend *Captain John's Seafood,* garnished by a giant lobster oblivious to its personal fate.

Beyond it, docked at right angles, was a second, larger restaurant, the longer, sleeker, taller *Jadran,* a former Adriatic cruise ship that in 1975 the Captain had sailed, with some help, through the Mediterranean, across the North Atlantic, and up the St. Lawrence Seaway, reaching Lake Ontario anchorage to the astonished stares of Hogtown's normally taciturn inhabitants. The *Normac* catered to a variety of customers; the *Jadran* was reserved for weddings, bar mitzvahs, company and anniversary parties, and banquets. Special-event revellers had sauntered along Captain John's Pier, mounted a steep ramp, and now whooped it up aboard the *Jadran.*

Beyond this brace of ships was the rippled inner harbour, fringed by the Toronto Islands, which on a map resembled a skeletal foot between the inner and outer harbours, but this evening to any gazer merely appeared to be a verdant sandbar. The island parkland was a sight worth absently contemplating from an open deck with your arm around your sweetie.

Couples and groups boarded the *Normac.* Taking a little tour once inside, they could note Captain John's extreme reluctance to abandon anything resembling a nautical motif. Mostly below the water line, the engine room and cargo hold had been merged into a dining area, including a blue-broadloomed floor, an oak and mahogany bar, captain's tables and chairs. On the walls were a rudder and oars. Chains from an anchor decorated the archway to the washrooms; even the stairways to the main deck were made from the ship's steel. The off-white walls of the main deck were replete with fishnets, charts, lamps, and oars from one of the lifeboats. Those handy anchor chains did double duty as ornaments for the coat rack and a banquette area at one end of the room. The original portholes and two picture windows afforded a harbour view. Diners could also ascend to a deck in which passenger cabins had been ripped out, replaced by a red, black, and gold lounge with its own galley and bar, each of the solid oak tables positioned next to a picturesque porthole.

While about a hundred or so diners enjoyed their lobster tails and surf 'n' turf platters on the main deck, Captain John himself, a tall, genial, dark-blazered figure, was engaged in his greeting duties on the *Jadran.* Even with about 30 crew on staff, the *Jadran* was busy as usual, but the Captain got word that the *Normac* was busier: to his satisfaction it had a full house. He hurried round the corner and into the *Normac* main-deck dining room to help with the seating or, as he called it in his Slovenian accent, the "things to do with the sitting."

Whether spooning the Captain's Manhattan clam chowder, delicately nibbling on grilled sole, or embarking on dessert cheesecake, the diners could vary their consumption by taking in the aquatic sights visible through the portholes. What they now suddenly saw surprised them. Something much larger and heavier than the ship they were on was heading straight for the side of the *Normac.* So the crew of the *Pequod* might have felt when Moby Dick, the Great White Whale, decided to drop by for a visit.

A man from Norwalk, Connecticut yelled, "That thing is going to hit us, get the hell out!"

A honeymooning bride from Miami screamed, "We're going to be run down!"

"You're crazy," said the groom.

But she wasn't. At the crash and crunch, the *Normac* rocked on its moorings. People toppled off their chairs. Coffee, cocktails, and dinner plates went flying or spilled into laps. Someone's baked potato sailed across the aisle and hit another patron.

Over by a window Captain John's friend, Det. Insp. Bill Bolton, who had been dining with an acquaintance, was taking deep gulps of relief, not wine. The wall next to them had caved in, sparing only their table.

All the lights went out.

At the moment of the crunch, Captain John not unnaturally thought that a bomb had gone off. In that instant, the Captain's reaction might have been summarized as "What the hell!" He had no time to think. The dining room's main entrance was smashed. Walls and bulkheads were crushed, and even the emergency exit had wrenched shut. It was the only way out – other than squeezing through the portholes and dropping bodily several feet into the murky harbour.

Captain John found a crowbar in the little unlocked cubicle of shovels and brooms he called his "workshop." He used it to pry open the bent exit door.

Elsewhere, every electrical circuit on the ship was popping and shorting, and water was rushing into the washroom. Darkness notwithstanding, the diners lost no time racing down the gangway to reach the safety of the pier, though not neglecting to thriftily take along their undrunk bottles of wine, perhaps exposing the Captain to a charge of failing to obtain a patio licence. While passengers wandered dazed, quaffing their wine for moral support, the pier soon was swarming with police, firefighters, and paramedics, not to mention reporters from the *Toronto Star* building at One Yonge Street, mere steps away. Two shaken-up ladies were taken to hospital. They were the only casualties.

A visitor from Timmins, northern Ontario, who had been trying to make up his mind whether to eat aboard the *Normac* when it was rammed, reflected that in Timmins, boats tended not to run into people when they were having dinner.

Meanwhile the ostensibly berserk apparent villain of the midships collision was shown to have been the *Trillium,* a paddlewheel excursion ferry, for whom the *Normac* could have been considered an inviting target, or perhaps another vehicle in a game of bumper cars. The *Trillium* had been scraped and dented for about 10 feet, her raised metal gate was twisted, her ramp damaged. But her injuries were as nothing compared to the *Normac*'s. The impact had driven the *Normac* against the street side of the slip, snapping off the steel braces that had held her steady, and two of them had pierced plates below the water line. Firefighters who put out a small electrical fire stayed aboard the vessel to pump out water, which was four inches deep on the lower deck, and had flooded the ship's bottom to the depth of three feet. The firefighters set up pumps to keep the *Normac* from sinking, augmenting them with plastic seat covers they jammed into holes. She was looking like a bathtub toy hit by a tidal wave.

For an hour or two the *Trillium* was wedged barnacle-like into the *Normac*. The pilot service tug *Terry S* pulled her back to the dock space beside the Hilton Harbour Castle hotel half a block down the street, where she should have been all along. The 81-foot city fireboat *William Lyon Mackenzie,* named after a nineteenth-century colonial rebel nicknamed "The Firebrand" for his temperament and the colour of his hair, slid in beside the capsized *Normac.*

Half his hopes and dreams were wrecked, but Captain John had not paused to brood, much less feel sorry for himself which, as a perennial extravert and optimist, he was in any case disinclined to do. He had to get the *Jadran* prepped for next day's lunch. The hungry had to be fed.

PART ONE

THE WAR IN SLOVENIA

Nineteen-thirty-eight was not a good year for Europe, though it was better than the years that lay just ahead. In March, Adolph Hitler, once a down-and-out dauber of Viennese watercolours copied from postcards, re-entered the Austrian capital, this time in glory. With the *Wehrmacht*, the German army, as a bristling escort, his triumphal motor tour took him through his modest birthplace in Braunau am Inn on the Bavarian border, perhaps summoning in the Führer fond recollections of happy childhood days. In Graz and other Austrian cities, flower-waving Nazi saluters ecstatically welcomed him; those who didn't want to were already in jail or planning to get the next train out. He'd issued his ultimatum; a rigged plebiscite had endorsed the Nazi takeover; Britain and France had dithered; Austria was his. Worse was to come. At the end of September, Britain, France, and Italy agreed in Munich to goose-stepping Germany's entry into Czechoslovakia's Sudetenland, where many ethnic Germans had long lived. The hapless and helpless Czechs hadn't been invited to the conference that was optimistically supposed to end Hitler's territorial claims.

In the hamlet of St. Ana, near the northern border of Austria's next-door neighbour Slovenia, 1938 was a happier year, at least for the family of Janez and Marija Letnik. On October 24, Ivan Letnik was born, their first son – a momentous event, since it had been preceded by the birth of four daughters: Marija, Antonija, Angela (who had died in 1931, aged a few months), and Kristina. It was no wonder that there were two Marijas in the family: it was the most common female name in Slovenia. In the peculiar way by which children acquire nicknames in a family, the boy was soon dubbed "Hanse," a diminutive of Hans.

On behalf of Hanse, and the rest of the growing family, Janez and Marija eked out a living from their farm, whose outbuildings included a gristmill and whose livestock numbered a cow, as well as pigs and chickens that they slaughtered for home consumption. Janez augmented his income by constructing barns and farmhouses. His own house was not convenienced by electricity, and water had to be fetched from a well. Janez grew corn, potatoes, cucumbers, tomatoes, and wheat that, like the grain of his neighbours, he ground into flour in his gristmill. They made sauerkraut; Marija bottled jams and jellies, and simmered savoury stews.

The land itself was kind, the fertile soil amenable to orchards and vineyards, abetted by a temperate climate: no colder than the mid-20s Fahrenheit in winter, no hotter than the mid-70s Fahrenheit in the warmest months. For himself and his friends, Janez distilled slivovitz, the potent Yugoslav plum brandy. Slovenes had always been famous apiarists, and even exported their bees, such as the Carniolan honeybee, native to Slovenia. Like many fellow beekeepers, Janez carved and painted his hive's entrance. The honey helped to nourish the family, as did another distinctive Slovenian product: pumpkin seed oil, later touted as a cancer cure. Janez roasted and crushed the seeds, squeezing out the green, dark, dense oil. Every little bit helped. There were no photographs of these domestic scenes. A trip to a photographer's studio was a luxury the family could not afford.

Slovenes were anomalous if not autonomous in Yugoslavia, signalled by their Westernized cultural uniformity: they almost all spoke one language, albeit in several dialects, and they were almost all Roman Catholics, their religion – and architecture – heavily stamped by Austria. Beyond such safe generalizations about the country were the stereotypes about its people, perpetuated by travellers, neighbours, and even the Slovenes themselves at the point where stereotypes merged with self-definition. One guidebook author, J.A. Cuddon in the *Companion Guide to Yugoslavia* (1968), commented a decade after Ivan Letnik grew up that, as South Slavs, Slovenes "have pronounced, well-rooted noses, firm jaws, a general strength and definiteness of feature, and highish cheek-bones. They tend to be fairer than, say, Serbs or Bosnians, and their complexions are lighter and their eyes greyer...." Two years earlier, Brian Aldiss in *Cities and Stones: A Traveller's Yugoslavia*, observed, "The Slovenes are humorous, quietly behaved, marvellous at ripping polkas out of their accordions, somewhat tight with money, and born skiers...." In their self-defined identity, Slovenes were honest, calm, reserved, disciplined, hardworking, conscientious, if a little melancholy. Of course, such grains of truth came with a lot of overly generalizing chaff. It would have made as much sense to say that all Canadians were submissive, modest, polite, law-abiding, tolerant, passive, and boring.

Slovenia was about half the size of Switzerland, smaller than Wales or, in Canadian terms, about one-fiftieth the size of Ontario. This small territory held lots of topographical variety. In the southwest was a Karst plateau of eroded limestone underlain by subterranean rivers, gorges, and thousands of caves between the capital Ljubljana ("lee-ooblee-ana") and the Adriatic. To the east and northeast was the fertile Pannonian plain, the boundary between Central Europe, Eastern Europe, and the Balkans, centred in Hungary, bisected by the Danube, and stretching from Vienna to Zagreb and Belgrade. To the west was Italy, together with Slovenia's sliver of coastline along the Adriatic. To the south and east was Croatia. To the northeast and north, respectively, were its much bigger neighbours Hungary and Austria. Most of Slovenia was hilly or mountainous, and half of it was forested: oak and beech in the interior, spruce, fir, and pine in the mountains. The linden was the national tree, and the edelweiss the symbol of Slovene mountaineering.

Where the Ivan and his family lived, near Austria's long border, was indistinguishable from the forests, meadows, lakes, and mountains of Carinthia, once a duchy and Austria's southernmost region. Although most people in Carinthia spoke German, some near the border spoke Slovenian, and German place names often had a Slovenian equivalent: the centre, Klagenfurt, was also called Celovec. In fact, some historians and linguists associated the region around it with the sixth-century liturgical and homiletic Freising Manuscripts, the oldest extant text written in the language. From the twelfth century onward, another duchy, Styria, had been a distinct political-administrative polity, and from 1867 until 1918 a crown land of the Austro-Hungarian Empire. The northern two-thirds held mainly German speakers, though with a sizable Slovenian minority. Those in the southernmost third, Lower Styria, chiefly spoke Slovenian, though German was heard in towns like Maribor (Marburg an der Drau.)

When Austria-Hungary collapsed following the First World War, the federal republic of Austria claimed the northern area's mainly German-speaking territory, including the city of Graz, while Lower Styria became absorbed into the new state at first called the Kingdom of Serbs, Croats and Slovenes.

One Slovenian contribution to Austrian culture was the high-stepping white Lipizzaner stallion, developed in the Karst region for use in riding schools in Spain and Austria and which became the symbol of equestrian Vienna. Austrian architecture came to mark Slovenia everywhere, then and in later centuries, especially in the handsome Baroque or Vienna Secession centre of Ljubljana. Despite what they gave to the Empire, and the enduring Austrian overlay on their own culture, Slovenes had rooted their ethnic identity in their language, which had been spread by the printing press and Protestant translations of the Bible. The Habsburg-sponsored Counter Reformation crushed Protestantism, but standardized Slovenian survived.

After the late eighteenth-century reforms of Maria Theresa and her son Joseph II, Slovenian was taught in schools, though Austria made sure that German, the language of the elite, remained the language of government, just as Latin was the language of the Roman Catholic church. Although Slovenian derives, like other South Slavic languages, from Old Church Slavonic, Slovenia did not, unlike Serbia, become Orthodox, nor did it, like Serbia, adopt the Cyrillic alphabet.

Slovenian, long the language of the common folk is, like Serbo-Croat, an Indo-European language that belongs to a South Slavic subgroup of Slavic languages, but with differences in vocabulary, pronunciation, and grammar. For example, it uses the dual grammatical number in addition to the singular and the plural. Some secular literature emerged during the Napoleonic interregnum. "Slovenia," Land of the Slavs, first appeared in print in 1844. Two decades after the continent-wide political upheavals of 1848, and the publication that year of the *Communist Manifesto,* Austria and Hungary because a Dual Monarchy under Emperor Franz Jozef: they shared foreign and defence policy, but each had its own constitution. Slovenia remained pressed under Austria's thumb.

Despite the growth of new industries, disproportionate numbers of Slovenes immigrated, mostly to the United States: Cleveland, Ohio was a favoured destination. Whether or not it was part of the nationalistic swerve from the Germanic to the Slavic, Ivan's forbears changed their name in 1885 from the German- or even Yiddish-sounding Lettnigg to Letnik, an uncommon name in Slovenia. In 1908, Austria-Hungary annexed Bosnia-Herzegovina in their resolve to wrench the Balkans away from the crumbling Ottoman Empire. Serbians, having liberated themselves from the Turks, declined to be part of someone else's empire, especially not one run by the Habsburgs. In the 35 years prior to 1914, a rash of Anarchist-inspired assassinations had struck down heads of states and governments, claiming the lives of a Russian emperor, French and U.S. presidents, an Austrian empress, the king of Italy, and the king of Portugal. In 1903, Serbian army officers hacked to death King Alexander and Queen Draga and tossed their bodies out of a palace window. On June 28, 1914, a clutch of hot-headed youths, no Anarchists but ferocious nationalists who sought to merge Bosnia into a Greater Serbia, mounted an accident-prone pistol attack on Archduke Franz Ferdinand, the Emperor Franz Jozef's nephew and heir apparent to the Austro-Hungarian throne. After several miscues, they managed to kill the archduke and his wife. Interlocking alliances clicked like a revolver in a game of Russian roulette:

Russia, Britain, France, and Serbia vs. Austro-Hungary and Germany. World War I was about to begin.

When Italy joined the Anglo-French alliance in 1915, many Slovenes who had enlisted in the Austro-Hungarian army, died on the frontline fighting on Slovenia's western border. In the month-long Battle of Caporetto, whose aftermath is depicted in Ernest Hemingway's *A Farewell to Arms,* and which took place on what later became Slovenian soil, Austro-Hungarian and German forces, aided by liberal doses of poison gas, routed the Italian army. The Austrians won the battle but lost the war. Anton Letnik, one of Janez's brothers, was recruited into the army and fought on the eastern front; he was captured in Russia and interned in a POW camp in faraway Tashkent. He never returned.

After the war ended, one consequence of the Treaty of Versailles was the creation of two synthetic political entities: Czechoslovakia, and the awkwardly named Kingdom of Serbs, Croats and Slovenes, a decade later rechristened as the Kingdom of Yugoslavia. Democratic self-determination for nationalities, especially in the collapsed Austria-Hungary, might have been an idealistic U.S. war aim, but the Yugoslav kingdom produced a crazy quilt. Although some thinkers had long promoted pan-Slavism in the Balkans, the new kingdom proved to be restive and fractious. Slovenia and Croatia, with their Western work ethic, resented what they considered Serbia's legacy of corruption and backwardness inculcated by the later Ottoman Empire. Nor were they reassured by the political chaos that was the norm in Belgrade, especially after King Alexander was assassinated in France in 1934. Meanwhile, the 1920 Treaty of Rapallo had given Italy the western part of Slovenia, including Trieste – a third of its prewar territory. In the mid-nineteenth century, the Austrians had built a railroad to link Vienna with Trieste since the latter had become the main northern Adriatic port. So many Slovenes moved there that it became in effect the largest Slovenian city. In the early 1900s, Trieste was a remarkably cosmopolitan city. Having chosen the right side in the First World War, the Italians proceeded to repress or purge any hints of the Slavic.

During the global economic collapse in the 1930s, Slovenia suffered widespread unemployment but, given the rise of German Nazism and Italian Fascism, that was the least of its worries. In April 1941, the month Germany invaded Yugoslavia, Adolf Hitler paid a symbolic visit to Maribor, a few kilometres away from the Letnik family's St. Ana. Maribor was the second-largest city in Slovenia and held one of the oldest preserved synagogues in Europe. As early as the Middle Ages, Slovenian Jews had been involved in trading and money lending, and owned houses, vineyards, fields, and mills. This relative prosperity ended in the late fifteenth century when, incited by the nobility, the Holy Roman Emperor Maximilian ordered the expulsion of Jews from Styria, Carinthia, and the city of Ljubljana where a synagogue was converted into a Christian chapel. Nonetheless, some Jews remained, especially in and near Maribor. Although many Austrians had left Slovenian after the end of the First World War, some of its citizens remained German-speaking.

Maribor was thus a suitable spot for Hitler to urge his enthusiasts to – in a statement attributed to him there – "make this land German again." It was a familiar refrain: take this good land away from the undeserving and barbaric Slavs. Nominally under German civil administration, for all practical purposes, Slovenia was occupied by the military. As Mark Mazower relates in *Hitler's Empire: How the Nazis Ruled Europe* (2008), the Nazis attempted to Germanize those they considered racially eligible in the countries they conquered. Among

South Slavs, Slovenes were the most eligible. Slovenian was banned for official use, and hundreds of teachers were imported to teach German to kindergarten tykes. Hitler's henchman Heinrich Himmler deported 80,000 unhappily relocated Slovenes to Croatia to displace the unreliable Serbs.

Hitler's expansionist fantasy met its most forceful denier in a half-Slovene named Josip Broz, later tagged Tito. He had been born in 1892 in Kumrovec, Croatia, near the Slovenian border. His Catholic parents had met in Slovenia; Croatian-Slovenian intermarriages were common, especially in the border country. As a child, Tito often stayed with his Slovene grandfather. When he grew up, he became a journeyman metal worker until drafted into an Austrian regiment just prior to the start of the First World War. Though a brave soldier, he lacked the proper imperial spirit and was briefly imprisoned in a Novi Sad fortress in the Vojvodina region of Serbia. However, his superiors devised a more effective sentence, sending him to fight the Russians on the Eastern Front where, now a sergeant major, he was wounded, captured, and sent to a work camp in the Ural Mountains. In early 1917, freed by a workers' revolt, he joined the Bolsheviks, the beginning of many Russian adventures that included captures, escapes, and – perhaps a combination of the two – marriage. By 1920, he was back in Yugoslavia, where he joined a fast-growing Communist Party that was soon declared illegal. A machinist in factories and shipyards when he wasn't being fired for inciting strikes, he got a five-year sentence in Croatia in 1928 for his incurable Communism. Upon release, he went underground, and spent a year in the Soviet Union, working in the Balkans section of Comintern, short for the revolutionary Communist International, before he was returned to Yugoslavia as Secretary-General of the Party. "General," not "secretary," was the alter part of his title.

In late August 1939, the Molotov–Ribbentrop Pact between the Soviet Union and Nazi Germany pledged that each would remain neutral in the event that either were attacked by a third party. A secret protocol carved Northern and Eastern Europe into German and Soviet "spheres of influence," to use the deadly diplomatic euphemism. Germany had overrun Poland, leading Britain and France to declare war on it, and Poland was unceremoniously split into German and Russian spheres of influence. Such events required Western admirers of the Soviet Union to tie themselves in cognitive knots. They were forced to defend a non-aggression pact between two nations that had been implacable antagonists in Western Europe, fighting for control of Germany and intervening in the Spanish Civil War. Moreover, one of the Pact signatories, Nazi Germany, embodied everything – capitalism, imperialism – the Soviet Union claimed to oppose.

It is a Serbian national trait to act without fear or thought of consequences. Serbia had been browbeaten into making common cause with Germany and Italy, but a patriotic military coup on March 25, 1941 deposed Prince Regent Paul, who had ruled the Kingdom until the assassinated Alexander's son Peter came of age. Yugoslavia hadn't been included in the Molotov–Ribbentrop Pact, which was convenient, since on April 6, German, Italian, and Hungarian forces invaded it to the thunderous tune of the Luftwaffe's saturation bombing of Belgrade. In stages, the young Peter fled to England as nominal head of a government-in-exile.

Among the Axis powers, Italy took over southern Slovenia and Ljubljana; Nazi Germany got northern and eastern Slovenia. Bits were parceled off to puppet regimes in Hungary and Croatia. By then, Hitler had occupied or controlled most of Europe. His larger objective became apparent when, in Operation Barbarossa,

Germany invaded the Soviet Union on June 22, 1941. Moscow now told Tito, that saluting Stalinist, to start fighting the Nazis.

In Slovenia, it hadn't been that way at the beginning. As John Corsellis and Marcus Ferrar say in *Slovenia 1945: Memories of Death and Survival after World War II*, "...the Communists, who were subsequently to claim all credit for defeating the Germans, started off on the German side, while the anti-Communist Catholics, after to be branded as collaborators, began the war as a focus of nationalist opposition to the invader." Both sides changed tack. As newly embattled guerrillas, Tito's Partisans were on a starvation footing, forced to seize weapons from the abolished Royal Yugoslav Army, or uncertainly rely on what they could capture. In Yugoslavia, moreover, the war was as much local as global, with a shape-shifting enemy. At first it seemed, or at least the British hoped, that Tito's Partisans might ally themselves with the Chetniks, an ostensibly royalist, conservative, and almost entirely Serbian force. But the Partisans were soon fighting the Chetniks as much as they did the Nazis. The Allies, principally the British, backed the Chetniks. In Slovenia, the battle lines were blurrily drawn between the occupying German Nazis and Italian Fascists; the Communist Partisan guerrillas under Moscow's control, who sought Yugoslav-wide power once the war ended; and Catholic opponents of the Communists and their ideology. Some of the last formed the *Domobranci*, the Home Guard.

Ordinary Slovenes were caught in the middle. Side with the Germans, Italians, or the Home Guard, and you risked bloody reprisals from the Partisans. Side with the Partisans, and you risked fatal revenge on your family and friends, or at the very least, deportation to work or concentration camps in adjoining countries. Though far from gentle occupiers, the Italian Fascists at least gave Slovenes a degree of cultural autonomy, albeit severely limited. Not so for those in the north, where the Nazis pre-emptively banned the public use of Slovene, dissolved intellectual or professional associations and exiled their members. Should German soldiers suffer domestic casualties, the SS resorted to their typical terror tactics: one killed German equals 10 executed Yugoslavs and it didn't matter in the slightest whether the Yugoslavs in question had anything to do with the killing.

Resolutely non-political, the Letnik family was going about its usual household business one night when the SS crashed through the front door. Between house and barn they lined up Janez and Marija, their daughters Marija, Antonija, and Kristina, and their son Ivan. On a stand they set up a machine gun.

Then, as abruptly as they arrived, they left, but not without taking Janez aside. He alone in the family spoke German. Like the rest of the family, little Ivan didn't have a clue what they were telling his father. It was, after all, the Nazi way: "Let others complain, we do not explain." But likely it was something to do with getting his father into the German Army: "If you carry a gun, you will be with us."

The entry of the United States into the war, propelled by the Japanese assault on Pearl Harbour, and even more effectively the fact that the Russian invasion had committed Germany to fight on two fronts, had given momentum to the Allied cause. At the Tehran Conference in 1943 the Big Three – Stalin, Roosevelt, and Churchill – agreed to support the Partisans with supplies, equipment, and parachuted commandos. In the Balkans, on the principle that the most effective enemy of my enemy is my friend, the British had chosen to side with the Partisans, not the cautious, sometimes-complicated Chetniks, who had only intermittently battled the Germans.

Despite many setbacks, by the spring of 1945 the Partisans had hugely swelled in number – about 10 per cent were Slovenes – aided by British and American bombing runs and arms-drops. They had rescued and evacuated downed airmen, and helped prisoners of war escape from German camps, mostly in southern Austria. The Italian army had to ring Ljubljana with barbed wire in an attempt to prevent the Partisans outside the city from cooperating with the underground resistance inside it.

By that time, the Partisans controlled large tracts of the Bosnian, Croatian, and Slovenian countryside, not to mention border regions of Italy and Austria. Ljubljana and Maribor fell; the German general in charge of the Balkans was compelled to surrender his army near Velenje, Slovenia. Eight days after Germany's official unconditional surrender, the Partisans won the last battle of World War II in Europe at Poljana, near Prevalje in Slovenia, defeating units of the retreating *Wehrmacht*, the Nazi-allied Ustaša from Croatia, and the Slovenian Home Guard.

Meanwhile, Tito had installed his men and women in Austrian Carinthia, uneasily coexisting with British troops fresh from their Italian campaign, as well as in Trieste. When Italy became *hors de combat* in 1943, German troops had taken over Trieste, only to be bombed by the Allies and under attack by Italian and Yugoslav Partisans. When the Partisans regained the city, they arrested hundreds of local Italians and anti-Communist Slovenes, interning some in concentration camps like the one at Borovnica, Slovenia. But within two years, Tito, pressured by the British and Soviets, had withdrawn from both Carinthia and Trieste. Slovenia acquired a short stretch of Adriatic coastline.

Wartime Slovenia had been spared such gross atrocities as the Jasenovac concentration camp near

Zagreb, where the Nazis and their cohorts from the fiercely Catholic, ferociously Serb-hating Ustaša systematically or randomly slaughtered at least 100,000 Serbs, as well as many Roma and Jews. The Nazis, in their comprehensive round-up of Jews – in Belgrade some were poison-gassed in purpose-made mobile vans – exterminated as many Slovenian Jews as they could find. At least a million Yugoslavs died during the war. A postwar enquiry put the Slovenia figure at about 90,000, including those who were drafted into the Wehrmacht and died either in battle or in POW camps, as well as those who fought in the Italian, Hungarian, or British armies – not to mention those the Communists killed just after the war. Some anti-Partisan Slovenes, at the rear of the retreating German Army, in the Home Guard, or just independently, had fled into Austria. Some were interned in camps; some were forcibly returned to Yugoslavia, one consequence of the Yalta Conference in the Crimea, held in early 1945. With Allied victory in prospect, Roosevelt, Churchill, and Stalin had agreed that citizens of the Soviet Union and of Yugoslavia were to be handed over to their respective countries, no consent necessary. In what became the U.K. occupation zone of Austria, German-allied Cossacks were turned over to the Red Army in towns like Judenburg. Many Yugoslavs suffered the same fate as Draža Mihailović, the Chetnik leader shot by a firing squad the next year. The more fortunate non-Partisan Slovenes escaped to other countries, notably Argentina. As for ethnic Germans, they – whether or not they had been Nazis – were driven out of northern Slovenia.

Because many writers and artists were Partisan, the Partisans became legendary heroes, their struggles and exploits depicted in verse, memoirs, comic books, and countless postwar monuments. Outsiders romantically idealized them, too. As late as 1978, the movie *Force 10*

From Navarone, based on Alistair MacLean's namesake novel, implicitly lauded them as valiant opponents of the Nazis. A more disabused view had come from Evelyn Waugh, whose 1961 novel *Unconditional Surrender* was based on his Croatian wartime experience when he liaised between the British army and the Partisans. The anti-Catholic Partisans did not appeal to him, nor had Tito's move in 1947 to nationalize private property. Tito was still a central-planning Marxist. As it turned out, he was not to be a Stalinist.

At first, Tito appeared intensely loyal to Moscow, second in stature only to Stalin among Communist leaders. After all, the first headquarters of Cominform, the Soviet-controlled organization of Communist parties founded in 1947, was in Belgrade.

The initial sign of trouble started with the speech Tito had made in 1945 in Ljubljana, in which he complained that he had been forced to withdraw from Carinthia. This seemingly innocuous statement displeased the wily and paranoid Stalin, who at that point was not ready to sever mutually helpful relations with his wartime Allies. He was suspicious of Tito's independent-mindedness, and his audacity in posturing as the liberator of Yugoslavia. Unlike other Communist countries, Yugoslavia had in fact largely freed itself from the Axis, with only limited, opportunistic aid from the Soviet Union. In 1948, after Tito's dissents from Soviet foreign policy and his territorial ambitions in the Balkans, the Cominform expelled Yugoslavia. The differences had become so personal that Stalin and Tito mutely traded assassination threats.

As Fitzroy Maclean, whom the British had parachuted into Bosnia to meet Tito, said in his memoir *Eastern Approaches,* "There was no telling what might not happen to ideas in the Balkans." Tito was the only national Communist leader to effectively defy Stalin, though he retained such elements of the Stalinist system as concentration camps. He parlayed the divorce into Western financial aid from the Marshall Plan. In 1950 onward, he advanced the concept of "self-management," which featured elements of profit sharing among workers in state-run enterprises. In 1956, Tito, together with Jawaharlal Nehru of India and Gamal Abdel Nasser of Egypt, founded the Non-Aligned Movement, a third force to counter the hostile bilateral blocs of the Cold War. Nationally, he had bound the six disparate nations of the Yugoslav republic under the banner "Brotherhood and Unity."

♦ ♦ ♦

For the family of Ivan Letnik, the war had been hard and, at moments, terrifying. As the Germans began losing the war, the pressure on Janez to join their army mounted and only eased off when his doctor certified that he was unfit for service, and even supplied medication to back up the excuse. Other demands were more easily dealt with: when a German soldier or, for that matter, a Partisan, wanted food the Letniks gave it to him impartially. Ivan's family was, after all, better off than city dwellers: they could grow their own food. In nearby Maribor, temporarily renamed Marburg, a German-run POW camp for captured Allied troops was located. The city, an industrial centre, had been repeatedly bombed, but young Ivan wasn't paying much attention. He did not hear about, or notice, the lurching, wagon-laden flight of the Home Guard toward the mountainous border, though he did hear the pounding boots of Russian troops marching to and from Austria via Hungary. Whatever these brutish battling adults might be doing, however they trekked back and forth across the blasted landscape, he was more or less oblivious: he was too busy being a boy.

Ivan was seven years old at the end of the Second World War. In 1944, during the last gasping expression of the Nazis' potty racial theories, he had been forced to learn German for five or six months of Grade One in school. As a reflection of changing political realities, he had to take Serbo-Croat and Russian. Just after the war ended, another reflection of political realities came when the government appropriated some of his father's acres. The Nazis had tried to take Janez's life; now the Partisans were taking his land for their unexplained collective purposes. It was progress of a sort. After Tito adjusted his state-ownership policies some years later, Janez was able to buy it back.

As in North America and the rest of Europe, Slovenia had a baby boom, and the Letniks took part. Ivan's sister Ivanka was born in 1945 and a brother, Anton, in 1946. Otherwise, home life remained the same. They still harvested honey and pressed pumpkin oil. Marija, as ever a good cook, made sure her daughters were well prepared to become good Slovene housewives. The kitchen was always stocked with freshly bottled preserves. Janez was tough, forthright, and always knew what he wanted done: if the girls misbehaved, they got the same spanking as the boys. A good provider, Janez was not the kind of father who romped with his children.

In 1955, Janez sold his St. Ana place and bought another amid green hills in the close-by, equally venerable, and slightly larger town of Lenart. Once destroyed by the Ottoman army, it had been named after St. Leonard, the sixth-century French hermit, patron saint of prisoners. Aged 15 or so, Ivan had ended his schooling at the end of the Slovenian equivalent of Grade Eight and, with blue eyes, curly, light brown hair and a sturdy jaw, was reaching toward his eventual height of 5' 10." Like Janez, he hunted deer, pheasants, and rabbits, though his sporting pursuits did not include a pursuit popular in rural parts of Slovenia: trapping dormice, the misnomer for grey, forest-dwelling, heavier-than-a-rat rodents.

In Lenart, his sister Marija had married Stanko Pintar, who carved and repaired objects and articles in a woodworking shop. Ivan began to work for him part-time. On occasion, Stanko would take him in a horse and wagon for an excursion of up to two weeks, as far as Maribor, sometimes close to the Hungarian and Austrian borders. They'd spend nights in customers' barns, lying on hay with a blanket over them. It was nice and restful.

It was 1956. The Cominform had dissolved and the Yugoslavs and Soviets had reconciled after a fashion, but Ivan had more personal concerns. During the first decade of its tense existence, Yugoslavia had begun to relax. Ivan didn't, though. After his father's experience during the war, and the equally unpalatable aftermath, he could discern no promising future for himself in Yugoslavia, even if its Communism was one of the milder Titoist sort. He wasn't alone. Slovenia was becoming depopulated of its young. For those who sought to leave, it wasn't easy: they had to get visas to go to Italy or Austria: if they left, they might not be allowed back. Ivan had his eyes on the nearby border. It was becoming more and more tantalizing.

A STROLL ACROSS THE BORDER

It was August 8, 1956, and Ivan Letnik was in a different country, though in many respects it looked like the one he had come from. He was trudging along with a backload of wooden carvings, baskets, sieves, and spoons from his brother-in-law's shop, posing as a humble peddler hoping to sell one of the items to a farmer. He figured that if an Austrian border guard stopped him, he'd tell them he'd got lost.

A month earlier, the ruse hadn't worked. Only his sister Marija and her husband Stanko knew what he was about to try. He'd threaded his way through bushes but, since they'd been cleared away, soon lost his cover close to Sentilj, the biggest, busiest checkpoint. He skirted the crossing where Austrian machine-gun-toting soldiers stalked. They spoke Serbo-Croat, looking for someone just like him.

He hadn't gone far before policemen stopped this unlikely-looking character. They marched him to a bunker, launched a barrage of questions at him, slapped him around, and shoved him into a cell. They prudently removed his belt and shoelaces, and stowed them with his wooden bits and pieces. Whatever he intended to sell, they were determined that it wouldn't be in Austria.

Back living at home in Lenart, he had to suffer his father's fury at his defection. But he was only temporarily defeated. Stanko and Marija were more sympathetic; they weren't any more optimistic about the Yugoslavian future than he. Once more he loaded up his wooden goods, harnessed them to his back, put a few Austrian schillings in his pocket, and at mid-morning set off for the border, this time by a route taking him an hour's walk south. It was a cloudy day. He only knew a few words of German, though his vocabulary was beginning to expand. Still, he couldn't give a satisfactory account of himself when, once again, he was stopped after several hours of trudging on Austrian soil. He had no papers — he could only get his I.D. when he was 19. Ivan Letnik was 18.

This time, the authorities inconsistently chose a different method to deal with him. Clapping him in jail in Leibniz, a mere 13 kilometres north from the border, they'd got a good laugh at his burden of woodwares. They appeared to think he'd just arrived on a direct flight from the moon. Whatever their instincts might have dictated, they didn't throw away the key, nor did they dispatch him post-haste across the border. They did detain this extraterrestrial for 15 days, trying to determine whether he was a criminally or politically undesirable. Deciding he was likely harmless, they gave him a choice: he could go to an internment camp, or he could join his father's cousin in Graz, Austria's second-largest city — both Janez and Ivan's Aunt Marija (his father's cousin, more familiarly known as "Mitzi"), thought he was still in Slovenia — or he could go to work on a farm. They didn't return his woodenwares — possibly thinking they were surplus to his requirements, or maybe that they could be of service around the jail.

Ivan quickly dismissed the idea of internment, and he didn't want to burden his father's family. He chose the farm. The farm was at Fohnsdorf, less than a couple of kilometres east of Judenburg, a picturesque town in the state of Styria, northwest of Graz. Judenburg meant "Jews' Castle", alluding to the town's origin as an Alpine trading outpost in which Jews had figured. So it was more than a little ironic that the Jews were expelled centuries later, and that during World War II, its purlieus had sheltered a branch of the Mauthausen concentration camp.

On the farm of Ivan's employer, life was not so different from his father's holdings in St. Ana and Lenart. He helped feed the dairy cattle and pigs, and went off with the logging crew. The farmer worked him hard, but fed him well. Austria itself was very different from what it had been during the short but punishing Nazi era. A year earlier, Allied forces had ended their occupation, and Austria had become a demilitarized, neutral country.

A month after he'd sneaked across the border, his parents had finally learned what had become of him. One thing Ivan didn't want them to do to sign a missing-person report or file a repatriation request. He simply didn't want to go back. From late August until the end of November, he worked on the farm until he got sick — something of an understatement. A tumour showed up on his neck: he had cancer. The farmer had insurance to cover agricultural labourers, so handling the treatment expenses was not a problem for him. For Ivan, the cancer was.

For six weeks, he lay under heavy blankets on narrow bed in a hospital close to Judenburg, then was transferred to Graz's largest hospital. In Graz, his Aunt Marija finally got to see him. To Ivan's doctors, especially one named Karl Reiner, he was a challenge: on their morning rounds they swarmed around him. He couldn't escape the conclusion that they were practicing on him. Besides removing a sizeable hunk of tissue from his neck, their experimentation included many blood transfusions and a massive bombardment of radiation, nine treatments in all. He lost all of his hair, most of his teeth, and half of the hearing in his right ear. Half of his face was permanently numbed and, because he was still a growing boy, his right leg now was shorter than his left one.

Apart from his stubborn determination to make his own way, he had a practical reason in not seeking to go home: medical treatment was bound to be worse in Slovenia. In any case, he was sure he was going to die and had resigned himself to the fact that his life was ending practically before it had begun. Thinking that he was only temporarily in hospital, well-wishers would optimistically ask him, "Where are you going?" He told them, "Six feet down." After four months, the doctors dispatched him to Vienna for tests.

The cancer was gone.

Ivan left hospital for the Graz home of Marija Letnik, an independent woman well ahead of her time who, even if she was married, saw no need to change her surname. For centuries, Graz had so many Slovenes living there that it, not Ljubljana or even Trieste, was practically the capital of Slovenia. A university city at the head of a valley, only 50 kilometres from Maribor, it had surrendered to the Soviets in 1945. He got to know it intimately, as well as its mild windy weather, strolling everywhere, sitting on benches to read newspapers and magazines, or the Slovenian books Marija had given him. The Schlossberg, its castle atop a hill in the city centre, had long been a Habsburg redoubt: Archduke Franz Ferdinand – he whose assassination precipitated the First World War – had been born in Graz. It was to the park pathways of the Schlossberg that the recuperating

Ivan would slowly proceed, and even more slowly mount the steep steps to the clock tower at the top that was crowned by a sort of architectural tricorne. It was his favourite place to go. There he would sit, surveying the handsome venerable city below, some of whose Old Town buildings dated from the Gothic period.

Ivan made friends, though he did not become acquainted with the nine-year old Arnold Schwarzenegger, who had been born on Graz's outskirts. For something to do while he recovered from his cancer treatment, and as a possible exit point, he volunteered for a refugee organization operated by British, Americans, and Canadians. Another good reason for him to become involved was that the group gave him clothing, margarine, and sardines, all of which he promptly turned over to Marija.

He wanted to put Europe behind him. In its postwar devastation, it seemed to him nearly an enlarged version of Yugoslavia. Almost as soon as he'd arrived in Austria, he'd applied to immigrate to the United States. At the refugee group's office he asked to be sent to Cleveland, Ohio, a sensible enough request because Cleveland was home to many Slovenes, and at one point had more of them than Ljubljana. Many of them, like Frank Yankovic, "America's polka king," had prospered. Unfortunately, America had no more need of Slovenes for the moment, though it was not expressed that way in the letter they sent him. In fact, they were preoccupied with another group of departing East Europeans.

Encouraged by putative reforms in Poland and Nikita Khrushchev's denunciation of Stalin, the Hungarian Uprising had begun in the third week of October. When student demonstrators marched on the Parliament, and tried to broadcast their demands over the radio, they were fired on. Violence spread – Molotov cocktails against tanks – and the government fell. Thousands battled the security police and Soviet troops. A new government declared that Hungary would withdraw from the Warsaw Pact, which the previous year had bound Hungary to the Soviet Union and its political allies, and promised multiparty elections. There was talk of state neutrality. This the Soviets could not tolerate.

Meanwhile, British, French, and Israeli forces had invaded Egypt during the Suez crisis, blunting any moral ascendancy the West could muster against Moscow. Nor did Yugoslavia's Tito protest when Soviet tanks, having briefly retreated, rolled back into Budapest to crush the uprising. Two hundred thousand Hungarians fled the country, most of them to Austria – 10,000 alone across the border one early November weekend – smuggled, or crawling under barbed wire. They were temporarily housed in improvised camps, one of them in Graz, prior to resettlement on five continents. It was the first major refugee crisis since the Second World War.

Over the next year, Canada accepted more Hungarian refugees relative to its population than any other country. An amended Immigration Act passed a few years earlier had given broad powers to the Minister and his officials to refuse or admit newcomers. Such ministerial discretion allowed the Liberal government to admit more than 37,000 Hungarian refugees, many of them heading for Toronto.

A refugee official asked Ivan, "Want to go to Canada?"

He thought, what's the difference? After all, Canada and the United States were virtually indistinguishable to him. It was all America. It was all non-Europe.

The relief group gave him money for the trip, including the impending ocean journey. He told Marija he was going to Canada. She told him, half in Slovenian, half in German, "You're totally nuts." But she gave him a big suitcase, though he had almost nothing to put in it.

He took the train the northwest to Salzburg, paying the fare himself, since he wanted to conserve what the refugee organization had given him. On the train he spotted a few seats away a man whose suitcase, like his, bore the legend *Canada*. Back in Graz, the refugee officials had told them to do that. He spoke to him in German then, realizing he'd made a mistake, tried out Slovenian. It worked. The man was named Franc Verdinsek and he was from Maribor. It seemed that other Slovenes beside him were going to this unknown country.

Graz-Salzburg was just the first leg of the journey. He arrived in Bremerhaven, West Germany, the Federal Republic, one of the busiest departure points on the North Sea, and boarded the *SS Arosa Sun*, one in a French-built, Greek-owned, Swiss-connected line of passenger ships, registered in countries of convenience like Liberia and Panama. It specialized in cut-rate fares for immigrants from all over; refugees, too, because it had recently ferried many Hungarians across the Atlantic.

As liners went, the 25-year-old *Sun* was small, but it was still a long way from the deck to the dock for Ivan, as he peered down from the upper-deck railing. Up to this point, he had not been homesick. Now, for the first time, he was overwhelmed by a sense of what he was leaving behind. It could almost be called a sinking feeling, one that he hoped would not be duplicated literally when they crossed the North Atlantic. The *Arosa* ships lacked stabilizers, fins mounted beneath the waterline whose changing angles counteracted rolls caused by wind or waves.

After a choppy crossing of the English Channel, the *Sun* paused at Southampton, but no one disembarked. Instead, new passengers were ferried out to the anchorage. With smoother sailing across the North

Atlantic than in the Channel, the *Sun* proved a boon to Ivan although, as befitted his humble station, his lower-level cabin had no portholes, and he had to share it with two fellow refugees or fugitives. But he cheerfully spent his refugee group-allotted $1 a day on Coca Cola, and bounded onto the dance floor at night, notwithstanding having one leg shorter than the other.

When the *Arosa Sun* arrived in Quebec City on August 8 after 12 days at sea, there was no mighty woman, in the words of Emma Lazarus poem, to lift her lamp beside the golden door. There was, however, a Customs officer to ask the homeless and tempest-tossed youngster what money he had on him. The question was easily answered. He'd been given $12 when he left Graz, and $1 a day for the journey. The refugee organization had also given him a train ticket from Quebec City to Toronto, and $5 for the two-day journey via Montreal. With him again was Franc Vevdinsek, his fellow passenger on the train to Bremerhaven, and his shipmate on the *Arosa Sun,* who was going on to Hamilton, where there were steel-making jobs. In Montreal, they sat in their disconnected car for hours, diverted by a splendid, if partial and static, view of a rail yard. They were waiting for another train to Toronto's Union Station to take them into their future.

Union Station was a Beaux-Arts cathedral with a block-long columned limestone facade on Front Street West. Adjacent to it, but buried beneath it, was the Union subway station, opened in 1954 as the southern terminus of a new subway line. Arriving after the featureless trip from Quebec City, Canada slowly flashing before his eyes, Ivan trudged up ramps from the railway tracks, his big but largely empty suitcase in his hand. He surfaced in the vaulted-ceiling Great Hall, 249 feet long and 89 feet tall at its loftiest, monumental and enduring in bronze, limestone, marble, tiles, and the translucent glass of four-storey clerestory windows, and marble underfoot.

Ivan was more preoccupied with figuring what to do next than he was marvelling at the Great Hall's grandeur, or at the long cornice that was hugely carved names: EDMONTON SASKATOON WINNIPEG PORT-ARTHUR NORTH-BAY SARNIA LONDON TORONTO OTTAWA SHERBROOKE LEVIS MONCTON HALIFAX ST. JOHN FREDERICTON QUEBEC MONTREAL HAMILTON WINDSOR SAULT ST. MARIE SUDBURY FORT-WILLIAM REGINA MOOSE JAW CALGARY VANCOUVER. He didn't note that Sault Ste. Marie was misspelled. Nor did he know where or what was Moose Jaw. A train destination apparently, but he was not going there, nor was information about where a homeless 18-year-old could go readily available at the ticket or baggage counters. There was no one to meet him, no names, addresses, and phone numbers to guarantee a friendly welcome — or any welcome at all.

He had nowhere to stay. He certainly couldn't afford to take a bed in the massive, opulent Royal York Hotel across the street. Wandering bewildered, he strained his ears to hear any language other than English. He heard a familiar one. He had learned German in Austria, and certainly it was easier than English had turned out to be. He approached the German-speaking couple and struck up a conversation. He told them where he was from and what had happened to him. Did they know of any Slovenes in Canada? Did any such Slovenes have a church?

As it happened, they lived near Bloor and Ossington Street and relatively near at the corner of Bloor and Manning streets, stood a Slovenian church. The kindly couple drove him there. The church was called Our Lady Help of Christians. That was all right. He was a Christian who needed help.

TORONTO THE OK

Was the mid-1950s Toronto that Ivan Letnik encountered as dour, dismal, and deadly dull as retrospective accounts would have us believe?

It depends who you ask.

The long-established, high-society coterie labelled "The Toronto 400" fashioned their lives in an atmosphere of material comfort, dynastic intermarriage, and inherited White Anglo-Saxon Protestant values as much as they understood them. But here is the testimony of Kildare Dobbs, the Irish travel writer and man of letters, writing in *Running the Rapids: A Writer's Life* (2005):

> In the early 1950s Toronto was a dismal place. Capital of Ontario, it was the seat of provincial government, possessing a large university and a polytechnic school. It was the centre of the nation's English-language communications,

book and magazine publishing, radio, television and telephone networks; and, together with Montreal, was also a powerful financial centre with mighty banks and insurance companies and busy stock exchange. An army of accountants gave the tone. With all this it was the butt of recycled Philadelphia jokes – "First prize – one week in Toronto; Second prize – two weeks in Toronto." Canadians from other centres called it "Hog Town" or "Toronto the Good." Calvinist misery reigned. The liquor laws wee wretched. To buy wine and spirits from the Provincial Liquor Commission (sole vendor), you needed a permit on which every purchase was noted.

Everyone went to church on Sunday in a hierarchy of religions: Anglicans, United and Catholic. The Protestants made Toronto Sunday a penitential day. The churches themselves, with few exceptions, were the ugliest I had ever seen. Catholics, so long as they attended Mass, were in theory allowed to have fun, but even for them it was a challenge, with bars, theatres and shops shut. One summer in the fifties on the beaches of Toronto Island a man was arrested for not wearing a shirt as he stepped onto a path. Another was charged with drinking beer in his own backyard.

Such appalled strictures against Toronto Sundays might have been a bit unfair specifically applied to the city, because the Lord's Day Alliance of Canada was a national, Presbyterian-inspired organization whose strenuous efforts helped bring about the federal Lord's Day Act in 1907. It wasn't only nation-wide recreation-seekers who chafed under its restrictions; businesses wanted Sunday shopping, and some factories wanted workers to toil on the Sabbath.

When a young engineer named Tony O'Donoghue arrived in Toronto from Ireland in May 1956, he recalls in his memoir *Front Row Centre* (2001), he was strolling along Yonge Street soon after arriving from Ireland in May 1956 and he struck up a conversation with an older newcomer, an Englishman looking for a restaurant. O'Donoghue remarked on how quiet it was. The Englishman commented, "Here they roll up the sidewalks on Sundays. All the Protestants are in bed, the Catholics are at Church and the Jews are in Miami!"

There may have been veiled WASP anti-Semitism in the sally of O'Donoghue's fellow newcomer. Toronto had long been prone to a moderately polite form of the disease, and a tacit or explicit Jewish quota was firmly in place in academe and the professions. Back in 1933, in the bowl-shaped park more familiarly known as Christie Pits, had ensued a riot following a baseball game – not between rival fans, but between Nazi sympathizers and Jewish and Italian immigrants. Anti-Semitism was a symptom of a larger chauvinistic xenophobia, even in so mild a form as that recollected by David Helwig, born the same year as Ivan Letnik, in his poem, "Toronto" (1967):

When I was born here
eating was done indoors,
and the only Italians
ran a corner grocery
where my mother didn't like to shop.

Toronto prejudices had its inconsistencies. In 1894, Toronto had elected a black city councillor, William Peyton Hubbard, the son of American slaves who had escaped to Canada. Aided by George Brown, the Scottish-born founder of the *Globe* newspaper and eminent Liberal politician – Hubbard had saved him from drowning in the Don River – he served in office for 15 years. In 1955, it elected its first Jewish mayor, Nathan Phillips *né* Rosenbloom, dubbed the "mayor of all the people." Until Phillips's election all Toronto mayors had been Protestant, and every one in the twentieth century belonged to a bastion of the city's business establishment, the anti-Catholic Orange Order.

Nineteen-fifties Toronto was a city of oligarchies, marked by their enterprises and endowments. First among them were the Methodist, music-loving Masseys. The founding father, Daniel, had been a Vermont-born blacksmith who set up a foundry in Newcastle east of Toronto. Under his son, the vain, parsimonious, but forward-looking Hart, the concern began making farm implements and moved to Toronto, flourishing with the help of the Conservative government's protectionist tariffs. After a period in Cleveland, during which he became a U.S. citizen, Hart returned to Canada. Under his four sons, the family company's combine harvesters, threshing machines, binder twine, and tractors became mainstays on farms across the continent and abroad. Having absorbed a farm equipment rival, his company became Massey-Harris. Massey's evangelical beliefs decreed he should spread the wealth in conspicuous public benefactions, like those to Victoria College in the University of Toronto and similar Methodist institutions across Canada, the save-their-souls Fred Victor Mission, Upper Canada College, and the grand musical venue Massey Hall.

Hart's son, Chester, bought a carillon for Metropolitan United Church, the United Church having been founded in 1925 as a mix of Methodists, schism-prone Presbyterians, and stray Congregationalists: it became the largest Canadian Protestant denomination. After Hart's death, Massey Foundation, presided over by Chester's son Vincent, funded the Hart House student centre at the University of Toronto and the namesake theatre and string quartet, a public lecture series and, in 1962, the brick restraint of U. of T.'s quietly elegant Massey College. By the mid-1950s, Chester's sons had taken drastically different directions. Tall craggy thrice-married Raymond, had became a Hollywood star, portraying such American archetypes as John Brown and Abraham Lincoln, and the sage Dr. Gillespie in the TV series *Dr. Kildare*. His elder brother, small, dapper Vincent, had devoted himself to service to the Liberal Party and international diplomacy: Ambassador to the United States and High Commissioner in the United Kingdom. Connected by marriage to the Parkins and the Grants – pedagogic and intellectual oligarchies – festooned with medals, honourary doctorates, and his own coat of arms, Vincent chaired the Commission on National Development in the Arts, Letters and Sciences (1949-51), its legacies the National Library of Canada and the Canada Council of the Arts, and in 1952 became the first Canadian-born Governor General.

The Eaton money came from consumer goods, not farm machinery. Its founding father was Timothy Eaton, a Northern Irishman who had set up shop in Toronto in 1869. His novel principles: no discounts and no credit but a money-back guarantee ("Goods Satisfactory or Money Refunded"). It was the start of a department-store empire that set up branches in other cities and mass-mailed massive catalogues across the Dominion of Canada and, at its height during the Second World War, employed more than 70,000 people. Eaton's flagship emporium was at the strategic corner of Queen

Street West and Yonge Street, abutting its great retail rival, Simpson's, which a Scot named Robert Simpson had started about the same time ("You'll enjoy shopping at Simpson's.") The Eatons' Methodist benefactions were less ostentatious than the Masseys'. Timothy's son, the knighted John Craig Eaton, donated the lands and funds for the Timothy Eaton Memorial Church on St. Clair Avenue West, more familiarly known as "St. Timothy and All the Eatons."

Si monumentum requiris circumspice.

"Little York," "Hogtown," "Toronto the Good," "T.O." Disabused visitors, dismayed newcomers, or frustrated locals alike deplored Toronto. When Mark Twain was interviewed by a newspaper in 1895, he observed, "Toronto is 12 miles long, one way, within the city limits; the poor live at one end and work at the other – and not a car on Sunday. These families are as exiled as if the Atlantic flowed between them, but as long as God and the clergy are gratified what of it?" In his *Letters from America, 1913*, Rupert Brooke sardonically commented of Toronto: "It is impossible to give it anything but commendation. It is not squalid like Birmingham, or cramped like Canton, or scattered like Edmonton or sham like Berlin, or hellish like New York or tiresome like Nice. It is all right. The only depressing thing is that it will always be what it is, only larger, and that no Canadian city can ever be anything better or different. If they are good they may become Toronto." In the 1920s a staple line for comedians was, "I went to Toronto last Sunday. It was closed." Ezra Pound reputedly addressed a letter to his friend Ernest Hemingway, then a *Toronto Star* reporter and convinced Toronto hater, "Tomato, Can." Writing to a friend in 1940, the writer, painter, and exile Wyndham Lewis called it "A mournful Scottish version of America." Writing a year later in *Quest, the Evolution of a Scientist*, the Polish physicist Leopold

Infeld comments, "It must be good to die in Toronto. The transition between life and death would be continuous, painless and scarcely noticeable in this silent town. I dreaded the Sundays and prayed to God that if he chose for me to die in Toronto he would let it be on a Saturday afternoon to save me from one more Toronto Sunday."

Toronto's motto was "Industry, Intelligence, Integrity," companion to Ontario's *"Ut Incepit Fidelis Sic Permanet,"* Loyal She Began, Loyal She Remains. Another, more cynical version can be found in the poet and legal educator F.R. Scott's "Ode to Confederation" (1957):

If you want to be righteous and rich
And to know you have God on your side
You won't find a cosier niche
Than Toronto can always provide.

Despite its apparent prosperity, Toronto had an underside of crime, poverty, and prostitution, some of it centred in Cabbagetown, a neighbourhood of cabbage-growing Irish and Scots migrants, much later the terminus for displaced out-of-work Maritimers going down a road that ended a few blocks east of Yonge, roughly bordered by north-south Jarvis Street. In 1973, David Helwig quoted a Second World War ditty in *Saturday Night* magazine:

Yonge Street for business,
Bay Street for class,
College for shopping
And Jarvis for ass.

Allan Lamport, whose term as mayor ended in 1955, was famed for malapropistic expressions of civic pride. "No one should ever visit Toronto for the first time," "Toronto is the city of the future — and always will be," "All this progress is marvellous... now if only it would stop." "Toronto isn't what it was, but then again it never was!" Silly as they sounded, each had a grain of truth, like his comment on the powers commanded by

Toronto mayors: "Being Mayor of Toronto is like being a Prime Minister – without a cabinet or a majority." In his decades-long municipal career, Lamport at times had favoured introducing a little joy into his joyless burg: he had fought to allow sports to be played on Sundays, and in the 1940 campaigned for the opening of cocktail bars.

Like its joyless Sundays, Ontario liquor laws were scoffworthy. The latest ones dated from 1927 during the latter days of the Prohibition era, when the Liquor Control Board of Ontario was created. Only the province could sell liquor, and putative shamefaced purchasers had to acquire liquor permits as they might a driving license. They next had to fill out a form, hand it to a clerk, get it stamped, wait for their order to be fetched from behind a counter. They then had to hide it inside a brown paper bag. It was not unknown for a clerk to chide, for example, a dignified well-brought up lady for buying too much booze.

Equally inhibiting – though people still managed to get drunk – were regulations besetting those who wanted to drink publicly and the licensed few who could sell drinks to them. Singing was to be limited, lest, presumably it led to orgies, and women were strictly segregated from men. Females were only permitted to drink in the presence of a male "bona fide escort" in a separate "Ladies and Escorts" room because, one assumes, hell would break loose if women drank singly or together.

Although drinking regulations were equally absurd in some other provinces, general dislike of Toronto unified the nation, the common cause of Atlantic fishers, Quebec separatists, and Prairie farmers. As the British Columbia humorist Eric Nicol wrote in *100 Years of What?* the year before the Confederation celebrations of 1967, "Clearly, if Confederation is to survive another hundred years Canada must find a national esprit de corps. Cohesion cannot depend indefinitely on hating Toronto."

Toronto had grown up in the tract extending from the Humber River to the west and the Don River to the east. Between the two was Yonge Street, which itself was to become a river of sorts.

John Graves Simcoe, the first Lieutenant-Governor of Upper Canada, who always stoutly refused to call something by its Native name when he could rename it after someone or somewhere in the Old Country, gave the street the name of his Devonshire friend and neighbour Sir George Yonge, who prudently never set foot on it. Gwillim, the maiden name of his wife Elizabeth, a diarist and watercolourist, became attached to three townships. The story that she named three other townships, Tiny, Tay, and Flos, after her three pet toy poodles was probably apocryphal: since the townships were officially named in the 1820s, the canine honour more likely belonged to the pets of Lady Sarah Maitland, the wife of Upper Canada's Lieutenant Governor, Sir Peregrine Maitland. In the unlikely event the townships got their names from Elizabeth's poodles, it would have conformed to the family habit.

Simcoe gave his family name to a lake; his own name became attached to a town, a county and, in Toronto, a provincial civic holiday on the first Monday in August. In 1793, he decided that the shoreline along a sheltered bay on Lake Ontario would make a suitable colonial capital and naval base. Simcoe wasn't the first to discern Toronto's possibilities. During the seventeenth century a succession of native peoples had lived in the vicinity, among them the Seneca, Mohawk, Cayuga, Iroquois, and Mississaugas. In the following century, the French had built a small fort, Rouillé, near the mouth of the Humber River – in vain, since the British conquered New France in 1763, obviating virtually all the territory that France had claimed in mainland North America.

Simcoe set up camp with his family, colonial officials, and the Queen's Rangers near the Don River. Spurning Toronto, its Native name, perhaps meaning "trees standing in the water," he called it York, after Frederick, Duke of York. The place was nicely defensible, especially if the defenders could control an overland route to the upper Great Lakes. One such route could travel north to Lake Simcoe, and then dogleg to Georgian Bay, which opened into Lake Huron. Steered in the right direction by an Ojibwa, Simcoe had a route blazed along an old portage trail on which the French explorer Étienne Brûlé had travelled to become the first European to gain sight of Lake Ontario – prior to a misunderstanding with the Hurons, after which they killed and ate him.

Sloping to Lake Ontario, Yonge Street tracked the watershed. Over the next few decades, settlements straggled along it, creeks were rerouted, swamps were drained – though not enough to avoid a nickname of the terrain it traversed, "Muddy York." During the inconclusive War of 1812 – unpopular with many Americans, to the British a sideshow in their war with Napoleon – conducted on land and sea, American troops attacked York, besieging Fort York and looting the town. They didn't linger. During the war, much of the United States was unassailable though, at the beginning, the British took Fort Mackinac in what is now Michigan, and held it until the end. A British expedition burned down Washington, DC including the White House, and made a major, though losing, assault on New Orleans.

In the years following the war the United States pursued a relentless westward expansion. Comparisons with Canada became routine. In *Sketches of a Tour in the United States and Canada, in 1857-58,* the British traveller Charles Mackay comments:

> ...Toronto, a thing of yesterday,
> a mere mushroom compared with

> the antiquity of Montreal and Quebec, is built upon the American principle, which loves the economy of straight lines, asserts the necessity of system, prefers the chessboard to the maze, and the regularity of art to the picturesque antiquity of nature. It is first the plan and then the city; not the city in the first instance, to grow afterwards, or to cease to grow as it pleases, as was the case with all cities more than two hundred years old. The streets are long and straight. There is no more crookedness in them than there is in Philadelphia; and they all run at right angles to the lake.... Looked upon from part of itself, Toronto does not greatly impress the imagination; but seen from the deck of one of the ferry steamboats it has all the air of wealth and majesty that belongs to a great city.

In the 1850s, the first railway was laid along the waterfront. Water by way of the St. Lawrence, Erie, and Welland canals was still the cheapest way to ship wheat, flour, and lumber to eastern Canada and the Untied States. This changed. In the later nineteenth and early twentieth centuries vast tracts of land and lots filled in with lake-dredged sand were granted to railway companies. On this newly exploitable land companion industries set up merrily polluting shop.

In a 1950 guidebook, *Ontario In Your Car* (quoted by Jamie Bradburn on the *Torontoist* website), John and Marjorie Mackenzie understandably do not dwell on what was unsightly in Ontario's capital. Instead, addressing themselves to the long-established or emergent middle class, they expatiate on the delights of the rough-and-ready sylvan hinterland.

> Toronto may be the capital of Ontario and the centre of population, but it is by no means the whole Province. There are those among you, we are sure, who are looking forward with anticipation to the lakes and streams of the northland, where the bass and trout are waiting for you, where you can hunt wild life with a camera or a gun, and where nature has not yet been moulded to suit the whims of man.

In 1957, the year of Ivan Letnik's arrival, Toronto's population was still well below 700,000, considerably less than that of Montreal – in their rivalries, one could fancifully compare the two to Moscow and St. Petersburg. Katherine Hale in *Toronto* (1956) noted "...to drive anywhere within the 240 square miles of metropolitan Toronto is to realize how few builders, in some cases architects, or the people who commission a building, have a clear picture of what the building has to do. So we have a jumbled city of promiscuous planning in which few sections have been laid out with any sort of design." Interested in wealth if not majesty, to use Charles Mackay's words, Fred Gardiner was about to rectify the problem. Three years earlier, the provincial government decreed that the York County towns or townships of Toronto, Etobicoke, York, North York, East York, and Scarborough, as well as adjacent towns and villages, would become something called Metropolitan Toronto, "Metro," with its southern boundary Lake Ontario. A well-off Tory, Fred Gardiner, "Big Daddy," became its dominant and domineering Chairman. He soon became the bulldozing proponent of expressways channelling motor traffic through the Don Valley and along the lakeshore.

Meanwhile, Yonge Street remained on the straight and narrow. East and west street numbering began there. In 1957, North York was a suburb. Beyond it, suburbs had been inexorably gnawing away at farmland and a hint of the downtown core's presence began at Eglinton Avenue. Just north of the corner was the site of Montgomery's Tavern, where in late 1837 the Upper Canada Rebellion had met its comeuppance after rebels staged a scattershot, scantily armed march down Yonge Street. Their leader was William Lyon Mackenzie, "The Firebrand," the diminutive Scot, Toronto's first mayor, who had long battled the Tory Anglican clique who ran Upper Canada, the Family Compact, epitomized by Bishop John Strachan, another Scot who had taken a different political route. Another Tory, Samuel Jarvis, in 1826 had joined other rambunctious youths who, inadequately disguised as Indians, had smashed the printing press of Mackenzie's newspaper the *Colonial Advocate*, and tossed its lead type into the lake. The city later named a street after him. At Montgomery's Tavern, troops had dispersed the confused, ineptly led rebels and burned down the tavern like an early enforcement of liquor laws. In 1957 Eglinton was the northern end of the Yonge Street subway line opened three years earlier.

Further south came Summerhill Avenue and on streets east of Summerhill and Rosedale, stood the glumly sumptuous, ravine-set residences of the not so idle rich. Slightly north of Bloor Street was the eastern border of Yorkville, a former village. If you turned east from Yonge, you crossed a viaduct spanning the Don River Valley and the Rosedale Ravine, whose lower deck was designed to accommodate the Bloor subway, yet to be built. Turn west on Bloor and you skirted the University of Toronto campus and the Annex neighbourhood with its big tree-shaded brick or stone homes replete with ample arched porches, gables, and turrets. The moneyed elite – including the merchandising mogul Timothy Eaton – had moved from their mansions on Jarvis Street. By the 1950s, their Victorian and Edwardian sanctuaries were subdivided into boarding houses and college frat houses.

Downhill and downtown came other main east-west streets: Wellesley, College (a few doors east of Yonge, the brick hockey shrine of Maple Leaf Gardens), Dundas (two blocks west was Chinatown) and Queen, the stonily impressive facades of the department stores Eaton's and Simpson's. King Street West, with its near-by newspaper rivals the *Toronto Star* and the *Globe and Mail,* offered a hazy equivalent of London's Fleet Street. Parallel east of Yonge, Bay Street was a similar local answer, this time to New York's Wall Street. South of Front Street, on which massive Union Station stood, Yonge crossed tangled rail lines and abruptly, anticlimactically ended at nothing much except the harbour. Yonge Street had passed from water to water, lake to lake.

IN THE KITCHEN

The kindly pair of German speakers dropped off Ivan Letnik at the corner of Bloor Street and Manning Avenue. Sure enough, a church: Our Lady Help of Christians.

Knock and the door shall be opened. At 609 Manning Avenue, an assistant pastor, Father Janez Kopac, together with a Brother Cyril, answered. Brother Cyril found an attic room for Ivan in a rooming house on Euclid Avenue, just behind the church: $14 a week for room and board, make your own meals in the kitchen.

Ivan Letnik belonged to the third generation of Slovenes to come to Canada. Emigration agents in Ljubljana contracted the first, mostly male generation — more a ripple than a wave — to become sweat labour on fruit farms and railways, to pave highways and shovel rock in mines. Some went to the Prairies and British Columbia; most headed for Ontario. A century earlier, a few had trickled north from Slovene communities that had started up in the United States. At the end of the Second World War, the arrivals were mainly spurred to

Canada by the Communist takeover of their homeland: young single men, former farmers, or former members of the Home Guard who had been less pro-Nazi than anti-Partisan. Women became housemaids, factory workers or, once married, homemakers, sometimes doubling as boarding-house landladies. Ivan's group, largely economic migrants rather than political refugees, included the family members of previous immigrants as well as the young men and women who had been stuck in refugee camps. Within a decade or two, they started credit unions and construction firms, became doctors and lawyers, set up family-run travel and real estate agencies, opened butcher and jewellery shops, mostly in Toronto. They formed sports and cultural associations, complete with all-year-round clubhouses and summer campgrounds.

The Roman Catholic Church was a constant presence. As early as the 1850s, the snowshoeing missionary bishop Frederic Baraga, though based in Sault Ste. Marie, Michigan, had preached among Ojibwa on the north shore of Lake Superior. Sharing several roles with social clubs, the church was many things to Slovenes: not just a place of worship but a community centre, but home to, or sponsor of, benefit societies and schools – pre-Medicare stitches in the social security net. Choirs as well as big weddings and banquets regaled by polka bands culturally bonded them. In Toronto, Slovenes heard mass at the downtown Our Lady of Mount Carmel Church, but in the late 1940s diligently worked toward founding their own parish, starting up a preparatory women's Sodality of Mary and a men's Holy Name Society. By 1954, they had hired a Slovene contractor to build Our Lady Help of Christians Church on Manning Avenue, the first all-Slovenian church in Canada. Priests like Rev. Kolaric had come directly from Slovenia, members of the outlawed Vincentian missionary order.

The day after Ivan installed himself in a room, he acquired a map, located himself on the Toronto grid, and registered at a government immigration office near Davenport Avenue and the street redundantly called Avenue Road. The staff there told him where to look for a job. One possibility was a centre on Jarvis Street, mainly coping with Hungarian refugees, but open to other newcomers. Within a couple of days the staff referred him to the Toronto Golf and Country Club on Dixie Road out west in Etobicoke, which needed a cleaner and dishwasher. He boarded the Queen Street streetcar to the Long Branch stop, where the golf club manager, a fellow whose name to Ivan's ear appeared to be "Jennikins" picked him up by car and took him to a genteelly gentlemen's establishment north of Lakeshore Boulevard on Dixie Road, on the nebulous western border of something called Etobicoke.

If Toronto's Native name meant "trees standing in the water," that of Etobicoke derived from a Mississauga word meaning "place where the alders grow." Etobicoke was part of Metropolitan Toronto though, unlike most of the proliferating city, the usual grid was often broken with treed residential crescents, home to bank managers and the like: you had to be moderately well-heeled to live in one of its solid quasi-baronial or faux-Tudor homes – although Etobicoke lacked the cachet of old-money, old-family Rosedale or newer-money Forest Hill, the soberly ritzy enclave just north of St. Clair Avenue west of Spadina Road. Many Slovenes had migrated to Etobicoke, especially in the Alderwood section; the Church of the Miraculous Medal, founded in the late 1950s, even had a Slovenian school. Ivan attended mass in the church, at first in the basement, though in the beginning he'd trekked overland to Our Lady Help of Christians at Manning and Bloor, ruled by the long-serving Rev. Jakob Kolaric. In southern Etobicoke lay parks and golf courses like Ivan's Toronto Golf and Country Club, though the borough touched bottom near the lake as a seamy motel strip.

As a keepsake, Ivan retained his first pay slip from the Toronto Golf Club: $48.22 net for two weeks' work. His new job might not have paid much, but he could room in what was the third oldest golf club in North America. With a curved driveway, abundant flowerbeds, and tall windows the clubhouse resembled nothing so much as a stately home.

The stately pile was only home to him for a couple of months. The Toronto Golf and Country Club closed in the winter. Jenkins or Jennikens (he could never be quite sure which) and his wife promised to find him another job; if they couldn't, they'd still let him stay en suite. But a kindred club, St. George's Golf and Country Club, likewise in Etobicoke's Islington district, had summer and winter seasons. The manager's wife drove him there, where he recognized the truth in the Mackenzies' comment in *Ontario in Your Car:* "The Lord's Day Alliance has left a strong indelible mark on the city, for better or worse, and many visitors arriving on the Sabbath, look in dismay at the closed theatres and deserted streets, and they ask: 'Where is everybody? What do people do with themselves on Sunday?' The answer is 'They are out playing golf.'"

The fortunate few, anyway. Golfers – "no theory of pessimism is complete, which altogether ignores them," wrote the poet Irving Layton in a poem of the same name – drove and putted their white pellets on a course designed by the renowned course architect Stanley Thompson, who'd been known for his fondness for steaks, rye whisky, and cigars; he had died four years earlier, having designed, remodelled, or constructed golf courses in Canada, the United States, the Caribbean, and South America. St. George's was consistently rated among the best golf courses in the world. Ivan slept in what could be described as a suite, carved out of an adjacent former farmhouse. Two weeks after he arrived his first pay slip from St. George's Golf and Country Club came; this time it was $13.09 for four days.

Ivan saw little of wider Toronto, or even of the well-kept glories of Etobicoke. He was working six days a week, and his shift as all-purpose houseman and dishwasher lasted from early morning till late at night. He earned $96 a month, no medical or pension benefits. He didn't mind: he was happy to have a job. On Mondays when the club was closed, the staff could seek recreation on the nine-hole practice course, though the 18-hole course was reserved for big events like the Canadian Open. Ivan golfed left-handed. In winter, he was in St. George's rink, a striped toque slung on his head, tidily sweeping with a broom and coasting a granite stone with a handle down a length of ice in the bizarre Canadian-liked sport called curling.

Nonetheless, Ivan spent scant time on the rink or links. He was to be found among three tall men in kitchen-white toques reaching up for pots, sieves, and ladles near the metal serving shelf. The brothers Robert and Nicky came from Switzerland; Robert was the chef, Nicky the sous-chef. Ivan climbed the ladder of promotion from pot-washer ("the lowest of the lowest you can be," he said later) to dishwasher to cook's helper to second chef. The cooks contrived a very United Kingdom menu: the ever-popular roast lamb, the always-present roast beef with Yorkshire pudding and for variety, Irish stew with dumplings. They only encountered famous golfers like Arnold Palmer when one of them mistakenly wandered into the kitchen from the changing room next door.

Ivan, no less lusty than the average young man, discovered that there was a serious shortage of girls in Etobicoke, especially ones who spoke Slovenian. He would go to a dance in church hall and find only married ladies. In the midst of this scarcity, he had to line up to ask a lady for a dance, and then only with husband's permission. Something had to be done. Ivan had made friends with a brown-haired girl, Ana Roškarič, at school in his hometown Lenart before he dropped out at age 15. They wrote back and forth. At his behest, she arrived in the summer of 1959 by way of Austria, where she had stayed with his hospitable Aunt Marija in Graz.

Now he and Ana were going to get married, and they had to be quick about it. As her sponsor, and in accordance with immigration regulations, he was compelled to sign a document promising that he would marry her within a certain period of time or she would be sent back to Slovenia. They married at Our Lady Help of Christians at Bloor and Manning, some 50 of Ivan's grinning workmates looking on. Since it was a Monday and nothing else was happening, St. George's sprang for the expenses of a modest but jolly reception.

Ana became a maid at St. George's. Two years later, the couple decided to move downtown. Ivan left with a courtly "To Whom It May Concern" reference on the St. George's Golf and Country Club's dragon-crested letterhead signed by its Secretary-Manager, T. T. Elphick:

> This is to certify that the bearer of this letter, Mr. Ivan Letnik has been in our employ as a Second Chef for the last 3 ½ years, and leaves us to-day bearing with him the goodwill of everyone connected with this Club.
>
> Mr. Letnik is an efficient and conscientious worker, and we feel no hesitation in recommending him to any person to whom he may apply for employment.

> We hope that his success will be commensurate with his qualifications as a Second Chef, and his character as a gentleman…

It might have been supposed that the couple would gravitate to western-bordering Mississauga, whose name derived from Native Canadians, the Mississauga tribe. At first a township and a suburb of Toronto, it was spawning highrises and highways. One rationale for its sprawling growth was the Queen Elizabeth Way, a highway leading to Hamilton and the Niagara Peninsula, and spearing north as Highway 27 to the federally-run international airport called Malton.

The Letniks' new home-and-business location was not, as might be expected, in a strip mall in Mississauga, but a small building housing a ground-level greasy spoon on Dundas Street West between McCaul and St. Patrick streets. Across the way were the Art Gallery of Ontario and the Ontario College of Art. Ivan had heard about the place from a German friend who was in the real estate business. It rented for $125 a month. Like innumerable immigrants before and after them, John and Ana lived above their place of business. Ana helped serve the customers, who sat on stools at the counter, or in window-facing booths. With 35 seats, the eatery dealt out breakfast specials, soup-of-the-day, hamburgers, and toasted Western sandwiches. Coffee was a nickel a cup. When he had to raise the price to a dime, Ivan was anxious about what it would do to business. Not to worry: he sometimes had a line-up at the door. He did a brisk take-out trade from retirees, art students and teachers, and printing-shop employees. He called his enterprise the Pop In – not to be confused with Pop Art.

Savings accumulated from the raises he'd gotten at St. George's Golf and Country Club went toward a down payment on the building. In 1965, he brought over his sister Ivanka from Lenart, and she worked with him, wiping countertops and doling out hamburgers. Ivanka was especially helpful in managing the place when he went to Slovenia for three months. He drove to New York and parked aboard the S.S. *France.* There was ample room because, at the time of her construction in 1960, the 66,343-ton *France* was the longest passenger ship ever built. Though jet travel was rapidly overtaking leisurely ocean liners, even government-subsidized ones like the *France,* he was in a mood to indulge himself. The *grande luxe France*'s elegance and munificent fine dining was light years away from a greasy spoon.

Once the *France* arrived in Le Havre, Ivan drove overland: Paris, Lyons, then over the mountains to Geneva and through the long Simplon Tunnel into Italy. Then he went via Milan, Venice, and Trieste into Yugoslavia and, at last, Slovenia. It was his first visit there in a decade.

He was happy to see everyone, and they were happy to see him. One of the first things he did was to arrange visas so he could take his parents Janez and Marija to Austria. In Graz, they had a reunion with Aunt Marija, thence north to the vicinity of Vienna, where his devout mother could visit the shrine church of Marija Cel, to Salzburg, and to a mineral-spring mountain resort owned by a woman his father had known, who had fled in Austria in 1945. Then it was Croatia and the port of Rieja in Dalmatia, reuniting with his brother Anton who was serving in the Yugoslavian army. Anton went back with them to Lenart so they could all meet as a family in their hometown.

It was the army — though this time the Yugoslav, not the German, one — that again caused trouble. Ivan had arrived in Slovenia equipped with the Canadian passport that he had gained after spending four years in the country; he was now a dual citizen of Canada and Yugoslavia. One day the police descended. They took away his passport and assigned a registration number for him to join the army. It was like a horrible echo of the travails his father had underwent during the Second World War when the German army had attempted to dragoon him. Badly worried, Ivan urgently appealed to the U.S. Embassy in Zagreb, and to the Canadian Embassy in Belgrade — any port in a storm. Obliged to report to an army office about his doings and whereabouts, he kept telling them that he was Canadian, not Yugoslavian. Demanding his rights eventually worked — and maybe the Canadian Embassy did help. He got his passport back. The authorities even admitted that they'd made a mistake.

♦ ♦ ♦

Since Ivan had come to Canada, Toronto had changed dramatically. A team led by the great Finnish architect Viljo Revell won an international competition for the curvilinear design of the New City Hall. Under Mayor Nathan Phillips, (1955-1962), and his successor, Phil Givens, central Toronto was being madly modernized. The city expropriated and razed what were, in Toronto if not European terms, age-old buildings and neighbourhoods. The T. Eaton Co., which owned most of the land in the vicinity of Yonge, Queen, Bay, and Dundas streets, sought to build a big new store, demolishing not only its old flagship, but also the pink sandstone Victorian edifice Old City Hall at Bay and Queen streets. They would have tore down the Church of the Holy Trinity near Bay and Dundas: Timothy Eaton's descendents favoured Mammon, not God. They were forestalled by public protest and by another mayor, the beekeeping William Dennison, who also kept the Gardiner Expressway from trampling old Fort York under its wheels.

Just as reminders of early immigrant communities were being eradicated, more immigrants were arriving. Typically, they were not contract labourers or refugee camp alumni; they — Italians, Greeks, and Portuguese — headed for cities, not mines, farms, and mill-towns, often working in the construction trades. Toronto acquired its first pedestrian crosswalks and new expressways. The man behind the expressways was the hard-drinking Fred Gardiner, since 1953 Metropolitan Toronto's first chairman. As Robert Fulford describes him in *Accidental City* (1995), "Fred Gardiner was like his expressway: big, ugly, aggressive, and effective. He bulled through Toronto, just like his road, brushing aside everyone who threatened to keep him from going where he wanted to go." When Gardiner took office, Fulford says, "The city required many things, including enormous sewer and water systems for the suburbs, but what it most obviously needed was a way of getting tens of thousands of people from the western suburbs into the city each morning and home at night."

Thus were born three distinct populations, so different as to be separate species. Some urban dwellers were complacently content or else chronically impoverished, and neither wanted nor needed to move anywhere from where they were. In a separate category were those who braved winter blizzards and summer squalls to get back and forth from highway-side highrises or suburban bungalows as quickly as possible. Over time, a third category was added: those mostly middle-class denizens of the inner city who wished their neighbourhoods to resemble bohemian Greenwich Village of the 1920s.

The city was rapidly growing, the car was king, and traffic jams were to be avoided at all costs. Traffic flow was tied to burgeoning suburbia, and the need of suburban dwellers to commute to and from workplaces. The future of the city centre, as John Bentley Mays notes in *Emerald City* (1995), lay "in blitzing the blight and stinking small-industrial zones, and raising from the rubble a new town of high-rises and parks, populated by well-to-do cosmopolites working in shiny, tall buildings that would say cosmopolisis to the world. His agents were to be, and were, the newest generation of planners and developers, who believed, also with undeniable sincerity, that the path to urban peace and private wealth would have to be cleared by bulldozers."

To that end, Gardiner bulled ahead with epochal projects, the Don Valley Parkway and the expressway named after himself. Begun to be planned in 1954, fully completed in 1966, the Don Valley Parkway was a sweeping, controlled-access six-lane route through parkland from east-west Highway 401 that required removing hills, clearing woodland, and diverting the Don River. Near Lake Ontario it linked to Gardiner's other massive expressway, which tracked the lakeshore east from the Humber River. Under construction by 1955, it was functioning two years later.

Encompassing expanding Toronto, but including much else, came political change. The long federal reign of the Liberal Party ended in 1957, when the Liberals were dethroned by the Progressive Conservative Party led by a prairie populist, monarchy-loving maverick named John Diefenbaker, he of the quivering jowls and head of tight white curls. Provincially the PCs were also in power under the moustachioed, Alberta-born John Robarts. In 1961 Fred Gardiner retired as Metro Toronto Chairman, and was succeeded by William R. Allen – they named an expressway after him, too. Queen Elizabeth had opened the St. Lawrence Seaway. A suburban shopping plaza called Yorkdale began, the first of many malls, each companioned by a giant parking lot. In the inner city, Yorkville began to imitate San Francisco's Haight-Ashbury: you could hear Bob Dylan, Joni Mitchell, Neil Young, and Gordon Lightfoot at the Riverboat coffee house. The flower-child wannabes waited for Godot dressed in bell-bottom jeans and paisley shirts. Syl Apps, a Member of the Provincial Parliament, whose verbal skills may not have matched his athletic prowess as a former Toronto Maple Leafs centre and captain, called it "a festering sore in the middle of the city," and Mayor William Denison said that "a few hippies and [U.S. army] deserters are Toronto's only problem." On City Council, Allan Lamport proposed to solve the problem by demolishing the neighbourhood and turning it into a shopping mall. West along Bloor Street, in 1968 the counterculture, utopian Rochdale College seemed to the Establishment to be little more than a highrise, patchouli-scented drug den.

In 1965, during the Liberal regime of Lester B. Pearson, Canada's new maple leaf flag first flew officially. Metropolitan Toronto's six townships were now called boroughs. Out west, suburban Mississauga, confirming its population growth and tentacular sprawl, became a city. The Bloor-Danforth subway line was extended, and a new one started, the University line, from Union Station to St. George Street at Bloor, paralleling a hospital-lined avenue and the provincial legislature of brick and pink sandstone. Wherever a subway line went, real-estate prices rocketed. In 1967, amid the Expo 67 world fair in Montreal and Confederation celebrations everywhere, the Caribana parade began its annual efflorescence. The same year the Toronto-Dominion Bank Tower rose, a black monolith on King Street designed by Ludwig Mies van der Rohe. It was the tallest building in Canada, a mercantilist Kaaba in a commercial Mecca. A Serbian photographer named Boris Spremo had landed in

Canada and, in Split, Yugoslavia, a cruise ship called the *Jadran* had been launched.

When John Letnik – as Ivan was now becoming known – had returned to Slovenia in 1966 on the S.S. *France*, a novel idea came to him en route. Once he arrived in Toronto, the idea grew on him.

PART TWO

THE CAPTAIN FLOATS AN IDEA

John Letnik decided it would be a good idea to start a floating restaurant. He was only able to articulate the notion to himself as "something different."

A shipboard restaurant was a quantum leap from a Dundas Street eatery, but John had inventive ways of substantiating his fantasies, even if there seemed to be madness in his methods.

Toronto had a lot of waterfront, but along its offshore length there was nothing remotely like a ship restaurant. In fact, there was no ship restaurant in all of Canada, at least one tied to a pier. Seafood, the Captain's thinking went, was a luxury item popular with tourists, which may have accounted for the presence of the word in the names of Chinese restaurants. The farther away from the sea, the more luxurious, and Toronto was far away. And what better to serve than food from the element on which a ship rode?

When John got back from Europe he began shopping for a ship. Used ships were not the kind of thing that could be found in *Toronto Star* classified ads. But he learned that a 125-foot, 464-ton ship called the *Normac* was wintering in the town of Wallaceburg, known for the manufacture of glass bottles and brass faucets, while its new owner, Donald F. Lee of Port Lambton, was figuring out what to do with her. Lee Marine had bought it from the Owen Sound Transportation Co., which had retired her after a 37-year run as a passenger and car ferry. She had spent a year shuttling between Owen Sound and Sault Ste. Marie, 32 years on the Tobermory-Manitoulin Island run, and four years bearing automobiles across the North Channel from Meldrum Bay to Blind River and Cockburn Island.

Built in Port Huron, Michigan in 1902, the *Normac* began its travels as a Detroit firetug named the *James R. Elliot*. After many years of putting out fires on the Detroit River, she had been sold to the Owen Sound Transportation Co., which converted her to a ferry and renamed her after Norman Mckay, founder and general manager of the company and captain of its flagship *SS Manitoulin*. Mckay was later drowned in Georgian Bay. It was not a good omen.

Deepwater Wallaceburg boasted of sports fishing, hunting and pleasure boating. John was interested in boating, but not for pleasure. Intrigued by news of a nautical hand-me-down, he got in touch with Donald F. Lee. Lee was asking $125,000 for her. The ensuing negotiations testified either to Letnik's patience or to Lee's desperation – probably both. Lee chopped the price to $50,000 but even then John couldn't afford it. At their next meeting, he brought a chequebook with him and bid $27,500. Lee accepted the offer.

John needed help to get the *Normac* ready for its journey to Toronto, and to that end enlisted her former Captain, Harry McNeill, and her Chief Engineer, Wilf Lowe, as well as a cast of volunteers. Lowe took the engine apart and reassembled it, cleaning every component as he went. Once it was done, the engine ticked over nicely. To document the momentous occasion when the ship got underway the prolific Wallaceburg local historian Alan Mann climbed aboard, as did Donald F. Lee and his sons.

A retired captain from Port Dalhousie that John found set about revving up the five-cylinder, 350 hp direct reversing Fairbanks Morse diesel. A tall man, he couldn't stand upright in the low wheelhouse. With little fanfare but many expectations, John and crew set out, following the St. Clair River to Lake St. Clair. They crossed to Windsor facing Detroit, a homecoming of sorts for the former firetug. They traced the Detroit River to Lake Erie, picking up the 26-mile Welland Canal at Port Colborne. Over about 11 hours, passing under bridges and riding eight locks, they dropped 100 metres sea-level lower than Lake Erie as they bypassed Niagara Falls and descended the Niagara Escarpment.

Reporting on July 25, 1969 that the *Normac*'s voyage was underway, the *Toronto Star* reported that Letnik hoped to permanently moor his ship either in Oakville or at the Canadian National Exhibition grounds. The truth was that he didn't have a clue where he was going to go. He was taking a big chance.

So where was he going to park the *Normac*? On the weekend he reached Toronto after their two-day journey and the Harbourmaster suggested he anchor out in the middle of the bay off the foot of Bathurst Street at the breakwater – he could get to and from his ship by lifeboat. Monday morning a better option presented itself. He docked behind the Canada Cement plant at Cherry and Commissioners streets in the so-called Portlands. He was able to disembark easily, which was convenient because, like the Wandering Jew or Flying Dutchman, he busied himself over next few months conversing with potentially feasible onshore hosts. The

CNE grounds were still an option or maybe, east of Toronto, somewhere near Oshawa. To the west, Brondy Harbour in Oakville, also looked good for his purposes. It didn't look good, however, to the Oakville burghers, who irrationally feared that a floating restaurant would attract dreaded hippies: they even raised a petition against his proposal. He decided that it would be unpropitious to start a floating restaurant in an atmosphere of local ire. Back he went to the Toronto Harbour Commission, to whom he had earlier appealed. They suggested the development-starved base of Yonge Street. There in the early 1900s the Toronto Island ferry dock was located and steamers took passengers to Niagara Falls, Buffalo, Port Colborne, St. Catharines, and the Thousand Islands. True, the street desert was becoming populated: ground had been broken for the *Toronto Star*'s new headquarters at symbolically important One Yonge Street, and the Toronto Islands ferry dock was a couple of blocks to the west. However, nothing else seemed in prospect. A floating restaurant would be welcome. They gave him a 30-day lease. He moved the *Normac* there just before Christmas 1969.

By then he had leased his Pop In, his Dundas Street restaurant, to a Chinese family, who lost no time in changing its name and menu. The *Normac,* its replacement, had arrived in Toronto in her Owen Sound colours. The Captain soon had her painted all white and then shortly afterward had the steel hull repainted bright red. On its funnel was emblazoned CAPTAIN JOHN'S SEAFOOD.

Early in the spring he heard of a ship restaurant in Boston, Anthony's Pier 4, and drove down to see how it was managed. Its owner, Anthony Athanas, had a personal history not radically different from his own. He'd come to New Bedford, Massachusetts, as a five-year-old with his Albanian parents and had worked his way up in the restaurant trade. In 1963, he'd opened his restaurant on the Boston waterfront, which soon became, it was said, the highest grossing restaurant in the United States.

Edified by Anthony's example, John was anxious to get started. He had a lot to do to make his bulbous two-tone floating convertible ready for the dining public. August 8 had always been a date for commemoration. On an August 8 he had escaped across the Slovenian-Austrian border, on an August 8 he had landed in Canada. On August 8 he opened Captain John's Seafood Restaurant. The *Normac*'s former Chief Engineer, Wilf Lowe, attended; John's mother, whom he said had never played favourites among her children, had journeyed from Slovenia.

For legal purposes and on his driver's license, the restaurateur was Ivan Letnik. On his passport he was John I. Letnik. At first, he registered his company as Capt. Normac's Riverboat Inn, even though there was no river in sight. But now he was not Ivan Letnik, or John Letnik. He was Captain John.

Captain John's was a novelty in a city desperately in need of touristic novelties. Unless they wanted to drive an hour and an half to Niagara Falls, the city's visitors sometimes had to be content with strolling around Casa Loma. Prior to the First World War the construction of this midtown neo-Gothic folly, which included marble-floored stables for the owner's horses, had bankrupted the financier Sir Henry Pellatt. Unless one was a devotee of architectural Victoriana and Edwardiana, the nearest thing to architectural viewing pleasure, a somewhat equivocal one, was Honest Ed's, the discount labyrinth which a marketing and promotional genius (no refunds, no exchanges, birthday bashes, giveaway turkeys) named Ed Mirvish had opened in 1948, rightly reckoning that postwar immigrants and the indigenous poor would need to buy innumerable cut-price items. Mirvish, a promotional genius, cobbled together a showplace at the Bloor-Bathurst intersection, a block-long facade festooned with 22,000 red and yellow lightbulbs.

Prior to the 1960s, a visitor's – indeed a local's – dining pleasure was largely confined to hotel dining rooms like the cavernous Royal York opposite Union Station, the King Edward Hotel on King Street East, or the Westminster Hotel on Jarvis Street, "Home of the Fabulous Town and Country Buffet," whose smorgasbord was Toronto's first. Further down the food chain, one could frequent middle-class establishments like Fran's on St. Clair Avenue West near Yonge Street (where at late hours one could observe the piano virtuoso Glenn Gould order scrambled eggs), or order a rotisserie quarter-chicken at the Swiss Chalet.

As for adventurous eating, this was an era in which a cookbook recipe might allow that a homemaker *could* daringly rub the interior of a salad bowl with a single clove of garlic. Ethnic restaurants (Greek, Chinese, Indian, West Indian) were few and scattered. Those with enough in their wallets could dine at the ostensibly French restaurant La Chaumière, or treat their daughters to a wedding feast at the Tudoresque parkside Old Mill in Etobicoke. If it was garlic that diners-out unaccountably wanted, they could go to Carman's Steak House, which a Greek immigrant named Athnaasios Karamanos opened in 1959 and where the garlic from the bread accompanying its steak and ribs could be smelled down the block. For Torontonians, it was a racy aroma.

Captain John's would not be a steakhouse like Carman's, or like Barberian's, opened in 1959 by an Armenian named Harry Barberian, and conveniently situated on Elm Street off Yonge. A little, but only a little, closer to the Captain's idea was Winston's, which a much-travelled Italian named John Arena, latterly a clubhouse manager at the Rosedale Golf Club, had started in 1966. With its gilded At Nouveau ambiance and red velvet sofas and chairs, permanently booked power-broker tables, it specialized in rich protein and richer clientele. What would he name it? To call it Pop In II was out of the question. It could only be Captain John's.

The mechanics of setting up the floating restaurant were complex. Before Captain John's opened to the public, the Captain's workers toiled at renovations and cleanup all winter. The initial bill now totalled about $100,000, counting purchase price, renovation, and new equipment to seat 94 on the main deck and 35 on the lower. When Captain John's opened on August 8, the Captain had to wait six months for a liquor license, missing the opportunity for a profitable New Year's Eve – even then he couldn't open on Sundays. He acquired potable water for his ship from a *Toronto Star* property and power from Toronto Hydro; trucks took sewage away. His customers parked free on vacant land a block east. After he had the top deck ripped off, and a new structure erected, he could feed about 260 on several levels. Below the waterline, he had the machinery, bilge pumps, and pipes from what had been the engine room. He merged the engine room and cargo room to make a single dining area, leaving the engine in place to preserve the nautical atmosphere. He renovated the main deck and galley. He installed carpeting and panelling. Over the upper deck he built an aluminum superstructure.

The Captain finished his renovations in 1972, a year after the Metro Parks Department opened a new island ferry terminal at the foot of Bay Street. His diners sat on commodious captain's chairs, but he provided no ambient Muzak, the better so he could take his customers' orders because the radiation treatment he had endured as a teenager having destroyed the hearing in his right ear.

In the mid-1970s he'd been telling one of his customers about that radioactive time when the man said a relative of his, Karl Reiner, was a doctor in a Graz general hospital. The next time Captain John visited Yugoslavia, he ventured into Austria and looked him up. He presented the doctor with a piece of engraved glass "as a token of my appreciation." The radiologist was pleased.

Throughout the 1970s, the customers flocked, greeted by a smiling host uniformed like a cruise ship captain or possibly the ambassador plenipotentiary of some Ruritanian principality. The staff was more modestly attired as jacketed cruise ship waiters and served celebrities like Bob Hope, who was staying at the Constellation Hotel out near the airport. Warned in advance of royalty's arrival, the Captain eagerly waited for him. When he appeared, the Captain got him in through the kitchen to evade the regular line-up at the door. Hope's big hat also helped him stay incognito in the dining room. He was very polite, with no traces of his wisecracking stage persona. After he'd finished eating, he was recognized. The autograph line formed.

In those years, Beland Honderich ("Bee" or "the Beast"), the *Toronto Star*'s President and Publisher, would amble across the street for lunch. Honderich, a one-time Mennonite farmboy and high school dropout in Kitchener, had steadily risen in the *Star* ranks from his days as a Second World War replacement reporter. He tempered the Liberal Party politics, sensationalism, and Methodist sanctimoniousness that had been the legacy of the man who'd acquired the newspaper in 1899, "Holy Joe" Atkinson, making it more suburban middle-class in tenor. His was a hands-on, vaguely menacing, seemingly omniscient presence. At lunch, Honderich, sometimes alone, sometimes with guests, invariably ordered Manhattan clam chowder and a Manhattan cocktail.

It was the decade of business lunches. The press flattered Captain John's and, lining up, came Members of the Provincial Parliament, Ontario Premiers, ex-Premiers, and politicians who wanted to be Premiers. Captain John's was a favourite with municipal politicians, too, like Mayor Fred Denison and Councillor Fred Beavis, a roofing contractor turned full-time city politician. In fact, the Captain was getting very chummy with municipal politicians and fund-raisers. Friday was his day for socializing at City Hall, practically a second home; he'd go up to have coffee or a drink in the councillors' offices, fraternizing with people like Frank Paznar, public relations executive and member of the Planning Board. The Captain became a director of the Convention Tourist Bureau with half the Bureau's expenses covered by the city and the province, he sallied forth to conventions in Washington, New York, Boston, and Chicago to show what the Queen City could offer visitors. He hired a Portuguese waiter named Alberto Figuera and in August 1971 an office administrator of Polish extraction, Jeannine Sullivan *née* Jamroz, who had an accounting background in the hotel industry. In the early 1970s the staff presented the Captain with a giant lobster. The lobster's shell became an increasingly dusty *objet d'art* for the restaurant, and its meat — there is oddly little meat in a giant lobster — ended up on the diners' plates.

In 1972, Robert Morley, the rotund British comic actor, might have dourly commented of Toronto: "This is a city of skyscrapers, tall black towers standing back on tiptoe, cheating about which is the taller. It is a lonely city, a drugstore city, where the cheap counter food is munched by sad, lonely women already preparing at six in the evening for bed and television." But, for Captain John, these were good years, at least for business, even if, while all the *Normac*'s renovations had been going on at the foot of Yonge Street, he was living in an apartment in Scarborough with his wife Ana and their daughter Denise. When he shifted his residence to the *Normac,* he used a little cabin slightly larger than a broom closet for night-time sleep and intermittent naps.

In September 1970, a year after Captain John's Riverboat Inn Ltd. set up shop, the city assessed Water Lot 1 in Ward 6, Yonge Street, at $7,750. It was disquieting that they assessed it as property, not a ship. The Captain protested, but the city told him that other restaurants would object if Captain John's was made an exception. As far as the Captain was concerned – and he was very concerned – his ship would always be an exception.

A SHIP CALLED THE ADRIATIC

Why should an enterprising Toronto restaurateur have one dining ship when he could have two?

The *Normac* gamble had paid off. The Canadian economy was booming and so was the dining business on the *Normac,* much of it from the passengers who piled off U.S. bus tours. However the little vessel couldn't accommodate big weddings and company functions. Hunting for another, bigger ship, the Captain found that Canada lacked passenger vessels for sale. He did hear of one, a ferry in Kingston that went back and forth to Wolfe Island, but was outbid by the Quebec government — though he never learned what the government wanted it for. He vainly sought a ship in Los Angeles, but was only shown one ready for the scrap heap: he had to content himself with staying overnight on the *Queen Mary,* the dowager liner that was now a floating hotel. He next set his sights across the Atlantic. He poked into what was on hand in Piraeus, the port of Athens, where he was only shown ships a fathom away from the scrap dealer. He had no better luck when he resorted to shipowners in Dubrovnik, Belgrade, and Ljubljana. But, on a Slovenia expedition, he learned that the Yugoslav state-owned Jadrolinija was planning to sell one of its Adriatic cruise ships, the diesel-powered M/V *Jadran*, Serbo-Croatian for "Adriatic," not to be confused with a much older, partly sail-powered training ship owned by the Yugoslav navy. Built in the Dalmatian city of Split in 1957, she was one of three sister ships, her ports of call were Venice, Dubrovnik, Corfu, and Piraeus.

After the Second World War, the Jadrolinija had restored to service surviving but damaged steamers for its Adriatic fleet. However, seeking to capitalize on Western tourists and their hard currency, the Yugoslav government had laid keel for three replacements. The sailing was not necessarily smooth on one of them, the *Jadran*. A passenger reported, "During dinner your forks, knives, and spoons would quietly drift towards your tablemate, and the glasses too. Or vice versa. And this vibration wouldn't help you falling to sleep either."

While in Slovenia, the Captain heard that the *Jadran* was being briefly docked in Rijeka. In a rented car, he hurriedly bumped over bad roads from Maribor to Rijeka, once a free port and briefly the Free State of Fiume, then the property of Italy, then of Yugoslavia, Croatian division. Government officials showed him the ship, surprised that he had shown up and hardly believing that he wanted to buy it. He did. But the year of dealing with Yugoslav bureaucrats was done by inches; it was not so much that they were incompetent, but they were slow, as he said, in their ongoing pursuit of "moving papers from one desk to another." From Toronto, he communicated by telegram. It wasn't enough. In 1975, while a maitre d' took care of business at home he flew across the Atlantic seven times in quest of his acquisition.

The Captain and the bureaucrats settled on a price tag of $875,000. He also had to pay for a crew of 16 to get his ship to Toronto from its base in Pula on the Croatian Adriatic. He financed it the same way he had financed the *Normac:* a loan quixotically extended by a bank. The way Captain John handled credit was a little bit like the way cable TV companies might handle it: all was well so long as cash flow covered the interest payments. Instead of new TV subscriptions and renewals, the Captain counted on new or returning customers.

The old crew walked off and the new crew walked on, most recruited from the cruise line: they were ready to work because they'd been laid off for the winter. He hired a captain named Pasko. Thinking in pairs, he had a supplementary captain, John Mann from Manchester, an experienced sailor who back in Toronto had been an invaluable source of assistance and advice in turning the *Normac* into Captain John's Seafood Restaurant. He'd taken Captain Mann with him to Yugoslavia.

He kept the ship's china, crystal, silver, and furnishings, but declined the linen, and almost all the 20 brand-new mattresses or, as he said, he "donated them back." It would be unwise to export bedbugs to Canada. He also left behind several gold-framed portraits of Josef Broz Tito, and a statue of the great man. For a de facto dictator, Tito was not especially greedy or acquisitive, but he was far from forsaking the perquisites of power — it was said that, prior to acquiring his own yacht, he sometimes appropriated the *Jadran* for private cruises. The statue was impressive, but Captain John regretfully kept it from the gaze of Torontonians, some of whom were expatriate Yugoslavs who had many reasons to dislike Tito. In the 1970s, guarding against threats, a Royal Canadian Mounted Police car was more or less permanently parked curbside outside the Yugoslav consulate on Spadina Road.

Captain and crew set out at 1400 hours on November 1 from Pula: intermittent cloud, the temperature a clement 18°C, a smooth sea. Chugging along at a stately 16 knots or so over the next few days, they skirted Brindisi on the Italian peninsula on the Adriatic coast. They passed through the narrow Straits of Messina between the eastern tip of Sicily and the southern tip of Calabria; in the northern portion a natural whirlpool might have inspired the Greek legend of Scylla the rock and Charybdis the whirlpool. Eluding such monster impediments, the *Jadran* passed Palermo, Algiers, and the Cap de Gata headland near Andalusia, Spain – all abeam, at right angles. They stopped at Gibraltar to take on water and fuel, with enough time to take in the sights of the Rock, which included the unruly Barbary apes, actually macaques, the only wild monkeys in Europe – unless one counted the more restive nationalities. A superstition had it that if the monkeys ever left, so would the British. The monkeys showed no signs of leaving.

The Mediterranean Sea was behind him. Ahead was the Atlantic Ocean. As the ship neared the Azores archipelago it began to pitch and roll in the swell, and Captain John spotted giant stone cones on the coast. Volcanoes: he had learned about them in school. That was one benefit of geography lessons: they allowed you to tell what you were looking at. For six hours in the city of Ponta Delgada, the *Jadran* restocked itself with water and fuel.

The time zones were changing, and so were the sailing conditions. They had expected bad weather, but nothing could have prepared them for the North Atlantic's stormy season. If Captain John fell overboard it would be just too bad: he couldn't swim. In fact, it wouldn't have mattered if he *could* swim. On November 11, the log laconically recorded:

CLOUDY – SQUALLY
VESSEL PITCHING VIOLENTLY INTO VERY HEAVY SEA & SWELL
SPEED REDUCED TO AVOID EXCESSIVE POUNDING

The next day the log reported that the *Jadran* was "pitching heavily & shipping water occasionally," that is, water flooded over the side. To Captain John, it seemed that his ship was more under the water than on it, turning it into a reasonable facsimile of a submarine. Captain Mann was a veteran of troubled waters, and said the conditions were the worst he'd seen in 25 years at sea. The crew was almost universally doubled over seasick except Captain John, whose stomach seemed to have been fortified by some form of internal stabilizer.

Two days later, they gratefully sighted Cape Ray, the southwestern extremity of the island of Newfoundland, which landmarked Cabot Strait. Avoiding rogue waves and granite St. Paul's Island, a notorious mariners' graveyard during the Age of Sail, they entered the Gulf of St. Lawrence, a nearly enclosed sea and the world's largest estuary: half of Canada's provinces adjoined it. They were pointed toward the St. Lawrence River, and Captain John was about to see the country in a fashion that would have been impossible any other way. Speaking of the St. Lawrence, the great literary critic Northrop Frye wrote, "The traveller from Europe edges into it like a tiny Jonah entering an inconceivably large whale…"

Jonah proceeded upstream past the Escoumins pilot and marine traffic centre, then past the mouth of the Saguenay River at Tadoussac about 15 miles west. Then it was Quebec City, where the immensely long river ceased its tidal ways. In Montreal there was much to do. For example, there was the small matter of clearing away the lifeboats, and cutting the bridge off both sides of the ship so the *Jadran,* all 295 feet and 2,650 tons of her, could clear the sides of the locks they were about to enter on the St. Lawrence Seaway.

Completed only 16 years earlier, this jigsaw puzzle of locks, canals, and channels allowed ocean-going vessels to travel from the Atlantic Ocean to the Great Lakes. The builders of it had created a lake by flooding nine villages in eastern Ontario to make way for a channel through the Long Sault rapids and permit new hydroelectric stations upriver from Cornwall, Ontario and Massena, New York. Having already navigated the Welland Canal at the Seaway's western end, the Captain was now tackling its eastern portion: passage over a channel bed only 27 feet deep – no worries, since the *Jadran* had a draft of 16.5 feet. Upstream of Montreal, they cleared six locks, three in Quebec, two in New York State, and one in Ontario.

On November 20, the village of Cape Vincent, New York, was abeam. Nine hours later, having left the Seaway for the wider waters of Lake Ontario, the *Jadran* anchored at One Yonge Street, Toronto at 0817 hours. They had journeyed 5,236 nautical miles from Pula, Yugoslavia.

Captain John parked the *Jadran* at right angles on the east side of the *Normac,* which was berthed inside a U-shaped Yonge Street slip open to the south. Just west of them were the docked Simpson tour boats and the *Trillium,* operated since 1975 on charter runs in Toronto Harbour. He bought air tickets so that his crew could fly back to Yugoslavia three days later. Dealing with his mail, he got an unpleasant surprise: a $1,000 speeding ticket, the result of *Jadran*'s hurry to herself itself next to another ship about to be lifted with her in a lock. Captain Mann advised him to pay the ticket and dispute it afterward. Mann's advice was sound. After Captain John sent a cheque and an explanation, he was rewarded with a nice letter and a $500 rebate.

The next problem concerned the water that was pumped from one ballast pump to another. The Captain was able to right her, but in the process caused the *Jadran* to list. He had to recall an engineer from Yugoslavia to right her again.

While the *Normac* continued to thrive, Captain John set about to – putting it mildly – renovate. Without the benefit of blueprints – they were lodged with the insurer, Lloyd's of London – he had the ship gutted and walls taken apart to install insulation and plumbing. In the two decks below the main one, including the engine room with its generators and eight-cylinder engines, he aimed to convert 355 cabins to 400 dining spaces, plus another 200 on deck in summer. The *Jadran* and the *Normac* were to have entirely separate kitchens and menus, but he managed to rig an electrical cable and water connection between them.

At the end of 1975, he turned his mind to a mission of mercy. On the night of Christmas Day, a 10,000-ton freighter, the *George M. Carl*, once the largest U.S. flagged ship to become Canadian-registered, was heading for Toronto Harbour, stuffed with soybeans. However, she turned left and missed the harbour by four miles, wedging herself on a sandbar off Sunnyside beach on Humber Bay. Two days later, he told a *Toronto Star* reporter, "I'm willing to come to the rescue." The *Jadran*'s engines still worked. With apparent seriousness a reporter asked: If all else failed, would Captain John buy the *Carl* and turn her into a floating – or beached – restaurant? The Captain replied, "I don't think I would be interested. I have my hands full right now." As it happened, crews shifted enough of the *Carl*'s soybeans to release her.

It was back to renovations. In the kitchen, past a swinging door in the main dining room, he put to use three Italian-made steamers and a big oil stove, then replaced the latter with electric. The city authorities wouldn't let him use gas, possibly thinking that he might blow sky high the waterfront and, with it, the highrise egg carton of the *Toronto Star* headquarters across the street.

At the rear of the dining room, the Captain left intact floor-to-ceiling, Croatian-made all-natural light-coloured wood inlays, which could be dismantled in three sections. They depicted in streamlined form the walls and cityscape of Dubrovnik, in the Middle Ages a city-state to rival Venice. As a piece of art it was, the Captain thought, probably worth more than the *Jadran* itself. To its left were more wood inlays, these showing a composite of a Serbian Orthodox church complete with a floor plan, ladders, posts, and a town clock. An allegorical woman held up a leaning beam.

On the west side of the room were linen-like curtains on windows facing an outside walkway, offering a view of the ferry docks. Exiting a glass door, one found in an antechamber a companionway — two open curved carpeted stairs leading up to a banqueting area, whose lack of windows was disguised with drapes. The Captain christened it the "Dubrovnik Room." For the east and west sides of it, he planned to set pillars with designs on frosted glass of the national costumes of the six Yugoslav republics — including, of course, Slovenia. Two of them, front and centre, were already in place.

By May, he had held a press opening, and hosted his first private function, a concert by a touring folkloric Slovene band followed by a dinner and dance. Then it was the dining public's turn, including his mother, on her third visit in about five years. He personally designed the waitstaff uniforms emblazoned with a dignified *J*: it stood, not for *Jadran*, but for John. Two years later, the spot where a statue of Tito had stood now held a bronze bust in coat and tie sculpted at her suggestion by the

Slovene wife of a Yugoslav diplomat, identified by a plaque: CAPTAIN.

The *Jadran* hosted varied events, one of them involving the showman Johnny Barbalinardo Lombardi, who in 1966 had founded the multiethnic CHIN radio station, initially to promote a supermarket he owned. He explained the station's name: "C is for Canada, H for happiness, I and N for international." Given to wearing a baseball cap, Lombardi, an ex-trumpeter, was a fixture of the Westside neighbourhood on College Street called Little Italy. Aboard the *Jadran* he now inaugurated the first of many politically incorrect bikini contests. A different and less heterosexual, event was mounted aboard the ship, the 1979 launch of the Village People's album *In The Navy*. The Village People, attired as American cultural stereotypes *qua* gay fantasy figures, bellowed out their biggest hit, "YMCA." About 200 fans and media turned up to hear it.

Less boisterously, the Captain and his wife were more or less amicably divorced in 1977; their daughter Denise was now 10 years old. It seemed to Captain John that Ana had always hated his being in the restaurant business and, although she had helped out at the Pop In, didn't want any part of it. It just took too much of his time. Although they had been separated for years, they remained on speaking terms. She started divorce proceedings; for his part, the Captain got an annulment through the cooperative priests at St. Michael's Cathedral.

It was 1981. At peak times, the *Jadran* and the *Normac* were getting packed houses of diners. Captain's biggest headache in the 1980s came during the winters; before freezeovers big storms would often hit, wrenching off the *Jadran*'s cable and the four ropes each on its stern and bow. But, apart from that, little had gone wrong. Little, it seemed to him, could go wrong.

THE LAW'S DELAY

The *Normac* was not upside down after the paddlewheel steam ferry the *Trillum* crashed into it on June 2, 1981, but it was far from happy, swamped in 24 feet of water. The 190 diners aboard the *Normac* hadn't been seriously injured. Nor did the 55 high school band students from the David and Mary Thomson Collegiate Institute in Scarborough aboard the *Trillium* report injuries, though they had a great story to tell their friends. Nonetheless, one didn't have to be an ambulance-chasing attorney to know that there were going to be legal aftershocks. The marine investigators combing the collision site the next day were the first sign of it.

Instead of returning to her dock after a harbour cruise, the *Trillium* had sideswiped an unmoving docked vessel minding its own business. To a disinterested observer, the matter seemed clear-cut. It was like one car backing into another parked in an empty lot. Which driver could possibly be to blame?

Wedged into the side of the *Normac,* the much bigger and heavier *Trillium* (138.5 feet long, 611.4 tons to the *Normac*'s 117.2 feet and 462 tons) had only suffered relatively minor damage. Not so the *Normac.* The *Trillium*'s bow had rammed it broadsides, damaging the electrical cables that fed it power. The impact had driven it into the stand-offs on the opposite side that had kept her in place in her berth and holed the hull. The hole was patched. With water rising to the table tops of the lower deck, the ship was pumped dry the day after the collision.

Two weeks later the Captain and a friend were in the *Normac*'s lower dining room when they noticed a little water seeping in. Then a lot of water. The Captain raced out of the ship to phone the fire department. It was windy, the harbour choppy. By the time the fireboat arrived, the *Normac* had sank.

The next day he stared at the ship's upper deck, the only part still above water, fighting back tears. He kept repeating, "That's my life." Newspapers were running cute headlines on their front pages: the *Star* trumpeted "Down the Hatch! Harbour Swallows Restaurant" and the tabloid *Sun* countered with "It's a fish and ship menu."

Captain John was not in the mood for jokes. He sued the Municipality of Metropolitan Toronto, personnel associated with the *Trillium* and, his lawyer covering all bases, the Toronto Harbour Commissioners. Filing in Federal Court in Ottawa, which handled admiralty and maritime disputes, he asked for $2,364,000.

His lawyer, Nigel Frawley of Paterson, McDougall, sought compensation for losses of business and good will, as well as the cost of raising the *Normac,* towing it to dry dock, and repairing it. A drop in the lake's water level raised part of the *Normac* but by the end of the year another legal front opened when Captain John conspicuously posted a plywood sign: "Captain John's dissatisfied customer of Aetna Life and Casualty Insurance Company."

Aetna, the huge Hartford, Connecticut insurer, had begun Canadian operations in 1960. In 1970, the Captain had got it to insure the *Normac* for $25,000, increasing the coverage in the following years. Although Aetna had sent an adjustor over, it had ignored his claim of $195,000 for the vessel's devastated contents. A judge had let the sign remain until the matter could be settled. This happened sooner rather than later. At the end of 1981, there was to be a cocktail party aboard the *Jadran*, booked long previously at the behest of John Hancock of Boston, an Aetna affiliate. The day before the party, Aetna suddenly glommed to the fact that its invitees would be strolling past Captain John's inflammatory sign. They instantly settled. The Captain removed his sign.

The settlement helped, but the Captain still had to pony up a deposit and monthly retainer to his lawyers, not to mention hefty deposits with the court while his lawsuit dragged on. The opposing side led a more cushy existence. In January, the Marine Club, an organization of shippers in Ontario and elsewhere, held its annual black-tie dinner for 1,655 members and guests at the Royal York Hotel, its President being one David Lomer Dudley Beard, the head of Beard Winter Gordon's admiralty and transportation law department. Beard was involved in defending Metro against Captain John's suit, now moving along at the law's usual glacial pace. "A sea of lawsuits prevent raising sunken 'eyesore,'" said the *Star* with a certain poetic licence. The Toronto Harbour Commission had grown tired of the *Normac* looking like one of the lesser casualties at Pearl Harbour on the afternoon of December 7, 1943, and began to apply pressure on him to have it raised. It was blocking the nice harbour view.

With the January ice crushing the *Normac*'s top deck, some onlookers thought the Captain was out of business. "If this continues much longer, I just might be," he said.

The city still adamantly refused to pay the cost of refloating it. Meanwhile, people had been gaping at it and taking photos – not a good inducement to dine in the adjacent *Jadran*. In March, the Captain dismantled at his own expense the *Normac*'s visible aluminum top half, including its funnels – about a quarter of the whole ship – that had stuck out of the water like a nautical affront.

In June, a federal Transport Ministry engineer cleared the expensively repaired *Trillium* to take, aptly enough, holidaying members of the Institute of Marine Engineers on a harbour excursion. Metro didn't have money for Captain John, though it was said to have up to $30-million of insurance coverage on its ferry fleet for any one accident. Metro certainly had enough money to equip the *Trillium* with a bow thruster so the marine engineers could go where the engineers wanted to. Recalling the collision, Captain John ruefully told a newspaper reporter, "It's a good thing that *Trillium* doesn't have a sharp bow or we'd have been cut in half." Robert Bundy, the Metro Parks Commissioner, whose department ran the ferries, called the June 2 accident "just a fluke which would probably never happen again. But if it does at least it will run into one of our own boats instead of someone else's."

Hired by a claims adjustor, the engineering firm Harold J. Wilkinson & Associates estimated at the end of August that $50,000 was needed to repair the kitchen and dining room, including the freezer and the waterlogged carpet. As the Captain's legal undertakings wore on, pulp and paper mills were kept in business by the voluminous correspondence between lawyers, legal secretaries, and court clerks affirming that documents had been sent or were about to be sent, and confirming that they had arrived or were about to arrive. The paper burden was augmented by copious exhibits that included elevation drawings, affidavits, certificates, letters, leases, surveys, plans, files, photos, diagrams, notes, operating manuals, studies, reports, logs, by-laws, inspections, notices, invoices, purchase orders, memos, models, photographs, postcards, sketches, forms, newspaper clippings, and applications.

In its statement of defence, Metro sought to shift the blame to the Harbour Commission; the latter "knew or should have known that to allot such a berth to Captain John's created a situation of peril over which the defendants...were unable to exercise any control." The Commission, it asserted, should never have assigned the same docking area to the *Trillium* and the *Normac.*

♦ ♦ ♦

Nineteen-eighty-two was a happy year for Captain John – at least compared to 1981. In August that year a man named Joe Olive hitched a sailboat to the *Jadran*, climbed up a rope ladder, and wed his waiting bride on the open deck, followed by a reception. That year the Captain travelled to Slovenia to mark the occasion of his mother's eightieth birthday. For the past decade he'd religiously phoned his mother on her birthday. To Slovenia he took with him a ring he'd designed in which was set the birthstones of himself, his brother, and six sisters. Now, posing for a living-room photo, his mother sat on a sofa, flanked by her sons Anton and the Captain, behind them Antonia, Kristina, Marija, and Ivanka (who now lived in Mississauga.) The Captain stood to make a speech, perhaps a little formal for delivery within an intimate family circle. But there was no mistaking the sentiment informing it:

Dear Mother, brother and sisters, relatives and friends!

On the occasion of this your 80th birthday, Mother, I would like to congratulate you not only on your age but what you have done in these 80 years. Look around you at your six children and their own families. They represent you, and because of you and the way you have brought all of us up, we are today happy, healthy, prosperous and last but not least a united family with you at the head of it.

We love you,

God bless you and thank you.

Afterwards, he told his mother, "This ring will go with you to the grave so you're never alone. We will always be with you."

After years of delay, Captain John finally had his judicial say. In Federal Court, mariners, marine engineers, and steamship inspectors testified during a 23-day trial presided over Justice George Addy. Their testimony retraced the unfortunate events of June 2, 1981. The *Trillium* was blithely splashing near its berth on the west side of the Yonge Street slip when things began to go wrong with its engine, despite the frantic efforts of its engineer. Alerted to the trouble at the last moment, Charles Colenutt, the Captain, was unable to reverse course. Dealing a glancing blow at Simpson tour boats, the *Trillium* ploughed into the *Normac*.

This hadn't been the first time that the *Trillium* had wavered in its docking duty. It had previously bumped the tour boats, and scraped a little paint off the *Jadran*. In 1978, Simpson had written the Commissioner of Parks and Property, which operated Metro's ferries, to suggest the *Trillium* use another berth. After the Commissioner checked out the *Trillium,* he recommended that it get equipped with bow thrusters to make it more manoeuvrable. Frugal Metro didn't do anything about it. Now Colenutt testified that, with bow thrusters, he could have turned his ship around before it hit anything.

It was not until March 27, 1985, that the Captain won a judicial victory of sorts. Although the *Trillium* failure to stop was likely caused by a mechanical problem, and not negligence on the part of its crew, what exactly caused the *Trillium* to go berserk wasn't clear, Justice Addy found. He concluded, "The burden of proof on the part of a ship which runs into another when moored or anchored in conditions of good visibility and fair weather is a very onerous one." Moreover, Metro had erred in not berthing the *Trillium* at the safer adjacent dock used by its other ferries. Addy rejected Metro's defence that the accident was inevitable, noting that "inevitable" was not synonymous with "unexplained." He cited precedents to show that Metro had to prove the engine failure was not preventable by the exercise of reasonable care.

Overall, he ruled that Metro was liable for damages resulting from the collision, but not for the sinking of the ship. As for the latter, he agreed with Metro's argument that in the two weeks prior to the sinking Captain John had done nothing to repair the damage to his ship. This, he said, amounted to "foolhardiness which would preclude one from considering the sinking of the *Normac* as a natural and direct consequence of the collision." Summing up, he awarded the Captain damages, later assessed as a pathetic $52,720.39. The bizarrely precise figure was a consequence of the Canada Shipping Act in which, following an ancient provision in maritime law, liability for damages was pegged to 1,000 gold francs per metric ton.

In gold francs or Canadian dollars, the sum came nowhere near paying for his legal costs and what it took to refloat the *Normac*. The Captain was still hoping to raise the *Normac.* In September, he asked for a loan from Metro Council's executive committee to do it. Meeting privately, they turned him down. Both the Captain and Metro were heading for the Federal Court of Appeal.

Meanwhile, the physical bulk of the *Normac* still lay unhappily submerged in the harbour, and divers had been sent to nose around the wreckage. In late July 1985, the Captain appealed to Metro's Executive Committee for a loan of $150,000 to raise it, though Metro's solicitor warned that a loan could invalidate the municipality's marine insurance. The Captain at least had one ally on the Council in the person of the long-serving Fred Beavis. In 1978, after the Mayor, David Crombie, resigned to run for the Progressive Conservatives federally, Beavis and fellow councillor Anne Johnston each had an equal number of votes to become interim mayor. The Council put their names in a hat, and Beavis won — it was as good a method of choosing a Toronto mayor as any other. However, Beavis only held office until John Sewell was elected two months later. Beavis now argued that Metro had a moral obligation to help Captain John's because his business had suffered. Metro turned the Captain down. Nigel Frawley, his lawyer, disgustedly commented, "They won't pay a nickel..." He had thought that Metro would pay the refloating bill "without prejudice" to the eventual outcome of the Federal Court's judgment. Said Captain John, "I've lost the whole summer, which is my busy season. I've had to lay off about 50 people and business is down 10 per cent."

On June 14, 1986, while a crowd watched, the *Normac* rose to the top of the harbour water with the help of Can Dive of Mississauga's 20 massive airbags attached to the bow and stern. Two months earlier, the company's diver had noted that the dining-room bar remained, but no bottles of wine. Since it was unlikely that looting divers had pillaged the ship's wine stocks, perhaps the Captain's customers had made off with them at the time of the collision.

Raising the *Normac* had been a struggle. In April, the Captain had thought the raising would occur in two weeks. In the event, it took two months. Even when the time came to bring it about, a city inspector had caused trouble about the lack of a permit for a crane, and a few days before they were to begin, the first crane company the Captain had hired for $40,000, jacked up its price to $125,000 to be deposited in a bank – this after he'd gone to the trouble of getting clearance from telephone, hydro, and railway officials. Hired through a referral from a friend in Niagara Falls, Sarnia Cranes demanded no deposit and did the job for $30,000. On witnessing the *Normac*'s resurrection, Captain John said, "I'm just glad it's over."

What remained of the *Normac* – which, lacking her superstructure, resembled a piebald canal barge – was towed to the foot of Leslie Street. She wasn't looking good, and best not to talk about its interior. But the Captain thought he could rebuild her. "It looks like a lot of work," he said. "Some people are very surprised when they hear that I want to fix her. But if you organize yourself, it can be done." The Captain told the *Toronto Star*, "That is my ship, my beginning." The *Normac* rested until the next spring, when the Captain got her cleaned out.

For his Federal Court of Appeal hearing, the Captain had a new lawyer, Harvey Siegel of Green and Spiegel. On February 24, 1988 a three-man panel unanimously ruled, their reasons delivered by Mr. Justice Mark MacGuigan, a former Minister of Justice and once a contender to succeed Pierre Trudeau as Liberal Party leader. MacGuigan found little fault in Justice Addy's view that Metro was liable for the collision, but differed from his finding that it was blameless for the sinking.

Captain John, MacGuigan said, should be held responsible as a restaurateur, not as a registered ship owner. The *Normac* was "technically a ship," but really a floating restaurant. To consider the Captain's standard of care that of a reasonably prudent owner of a ship at sea was "highly excessive." As for the contention that two weeks had broken the causal link between collision and sinking, MacGuigan said that nothing the Captain had done or failed to do had jeopardized the ship. Neither did he fault the Captain for not raising the ship promptly, as Metro's lawyer had claimed he could have done. He noted that less than a month before the sinking, the *Normac*'s market value was $450,000, and that the cost of raising and refloating her ranged from $324,000 to $890,000. "The economic cost of bridging the evidence gap appears to me to be so disproportionate as to be impracticable," he stated. Less cumbrously put, this meant that he thought that raising her would cost more than the ship was worth. After all this, he held that Metro was liable for 75, not 100 per cent, of damages, appearing to suggest that the Captain had been partly negligent, but not so much as to absolve Metro from mainly causing the *Normac* from sinking to the bottom.

"I'm very pleased, it was a long road," the Captain told the press.

David Beard of Beard, Winter thought the decision should be appealed to the Supreme Court. His advice was taken. Metro filed an appeal, which the Supreme Court agreed to hear. Then, thinking better of it, Metro settled for $1.46 million – the Captain's legal costs swallowed more than half of it.

Although the Captain had scant interest in legal technicalities, his lawyer Harvey Siegel thought that the Federal Court's decision was something of a landmark in Canadian law. He called it "a textbook on tort," (a tort being a wrongful act or an infringement of a right, except under a contract, that leads to legal liability). He told *Lawyer's Weekly* that the Federal Court had shifted the burden of proving a negligent act *didn't* cause damages to the plaintiff, (in this case Captain John), to a tortfeasor (someone who commits a tort, in this case Metro.) Although the Municipality of Metropolitan Toronto had been called many uncomplimentary things in its day, it might have been the first time that it had been termed a "tortfeasor." In Siegel's view, the Federal Court had adopted what was called a "reverse onus." In this case, Metro had to prove that the collision didn't cause the ship to sink two weeks later.

After he collected his Federal Court of Appeal settlement, the Captain had many plans. One of them was to turn the *Jadran* into a 70-room luxury hotel, for which purpose he had cabins ripped out. Another prospect was even more tantalizing. Invited to a social function at the Harbour Commission headquarters, he met visitors from Cleveland, who invited him to move the refurbished *Normac* there. Seizing on the idea, the Captain thought he might later sell it in Cleveland, and then use the proceeds to renovate the *Jadran*. No sooner was the Cleveland move said than it was done. He had the *Normac* towed across Lake Ontario, the Welland Canal, and Lake Erie, reversing the route that the *Normac* had taken to Toronto. In June 1989, two decades after the *Normac*'s Toronto-bound voyage, he opened it as a floating restaurant.

In 1984 the Captain designed a penthouse-like apartment on the top deck of the *Jadran*. Ripping out cabins, and cutting sheets of aluminum with the crew he'd hired, he created up a short flight of stairs an airy, bright open space, windowless but with three expansive skylights. In the front was a living room and tiny kitchen off it, in the centre a king-size bed, and at the back a bathroom with a big Jacuzzi.

On August 21, 1989, near the foot of Spadina Avenue west of Captain John's, a comical "Zingy Dinghy" boat race was held, involving craft fashioned from thousands of two-litre milk cartons. They competed for prizes like the "Sink or Swim" and "Leonardo da Vinci" awards. The competing vessels, with names like the *Ratt Trap* and the *Exxon Valdez*, which a *Toronto Star* reporter described as "a gerbil ferris wheel," often capsized or, alternatively, rammed one another. The *Trillium* did not compete.

THE COST OF STAYING AFLOAT

Almost ever since he gratefully docked the *Normac* at the foot of Yonge Street in 1970, Captain John had been saddled with a festering fiscal sore. The sore stemmed from a single, ostensibly simple question: was any vessel he docked there a building or a ship? For Captain Normac's Riverboat Inn Ltd., the legal name under which he operated, it was a question of fish or foul. Toronto's tax authorities said it was a building; Captain John said it was a ship.

This mattered, because if the *Normac* or the *Jadran* was a building and not a ship, the city could charge him property tax in addition to docking fees. He paid docking fees to the Harbour Commission. After 1999, when the Harbour Commission was reconstituted as the Port Authority, the fees eventually amounted to a monthly $2,500, to which was later added $2,700 a month for the uncurbed cement "sidewalk" that ran the length of the *Jadran*'s berth. For the 1970 taxation year, the year after the *Normac* anchored, Metropolitan Toronto assessed the Captain's property at a modest $7,750; in 1976, the year after the *Jadran* joined her, the assessment was $36,501. By 1982, the year after the *Trillium* rammed the *Normac,* it was $89,900. In the 1990s, after the Captain's tax bill had doubled, it was reduced upon his appeal. But by 2007 he was paying $36,000 a year in taxes.

Over the years, some of the Captain's friends and sometime diners were members of Metro Council, including Fred Beavis, Joseph Piccinnini, Chris Korwin-Kuczynski, Tony O'Donaghue, and Art Eggleton, Toronto mayor between 1980 and 1991, the longest serving mayor in the city's history, and later a federal Liberal cabinet minister and Senator. Korwin-Kuczynski was an honorary Captain of the Canadian Navy who opposed a 1996 municipal bill that banned smoking in restaurants and bars. But none of these politicians could provide practical assistance during his legal struggles in the wake of the *Trillium*'s collision with the *Normac* – much less his property-taxation wrangles. The city's amalgamation in 1998 made no difference to the Captain's situation.

In 2007, the Captain as usual sought redress in court. The provincial Assessment Act said that "real property" included "all structures" on the property. To buttress the Captain's case, his lawyer, Jeff G. Cowan, cited a ruling by Lord Denning, a British judge famous for his tart and plainspoken concision. In Cardiff Rating Authority v. Guest, Keen Baldwin's Iron & Steel Co. Ltd., Denning had stated, "A structure is something which is constructed, but not everything which is constructed is a structure. A ship, for instance, is constructed, but is not a structure. A structure is something of substantial size which is built up from component parts and intended to remain permanently on a permanent foundation." Some objects that are constructed are merely "in the nature of a structure" without actually being one, Denning ruled. "This definition fitted the *Jadran,*" Cowan argued. Which meant that it was not "real property," and shouldn't be assessed.

Justice Laurence Pattillo didn't beg to differ. He forthrightly ruled that the Municipal Property Assessment Corp. had the right to assess it so the city could levy taxes. He noted that the ship hadn't moved since the mid-1970s, probably couldn't move without assistance, and had permanent water, sewer and electricity connections to shore. Although the ship floated on water, it still occupied the land on the lakebed. Although the Justice didn't mention it, some people believed that the *Jadran* was embedded in concrete on the lake bottom. But, as Captain John told a newspaper reporter, "I hope it's afloat – if it's not, I'm in trouble." The motor has been disassembled but, "If I loosen the ropes, I don't need a motor to move me away; the wind will do it. In the early days, we had much bigger storms in the lakes than recently. I spent days just watching the ropes, because she's free-floating. Many times the ropes snapped."

Patillo further noted that there was no way any other object could occupy the *Jadran*'s space. He neglected to mention that the *Trillium* had once shared space – albeit briefly – with the *Normac* and the *Jadran*. Plainly, waterways were not land ways. Captain John was disgusted. "When the *Normac* was sitting on the bottom then the city had a right to charge me realty tax!" he snorted.

The Captain appealed. In March 2009 a panel of three judges rejected his plea. It ruled that the *Jadran* was a structure, despite the lack of a foundation, because it was moored permanently. Moreover, the ship occupied not just the water, but the lakebed under the water, which was "land" for the purpose of property assessment. To add financial insult to injury, the court ordered Captain John to pay $7,500 in legal costs to the

Municipal Property Assessment Corporation. He wasn't granted leave to appeal. "I'm back to square one," he told a reporter. There the matter rested, or floated.

The Captain's financial tribulations were relieved by private pleasures and public honours. On October 24, 1992 – as it happened, the Captain's birthday – his daughter Denise, with a huge bridal train, married Robert Cable who, through his mother, was a third-generation Slovene-American from Cleveland. At the end of the service in St. Michael's Cathedral, they stepped into a waiting carriage drawn by a white horse.

In the 1990s, as if to emphasize the Captain's prime real estate, the city embedded in bronze in the sidewalk a legend leading west from the *Jadran*'s anchorage: This Is The Start of Yonge Street 0 km TORONTO 13 km NORTH YORK 26 km RICHMOND HILL 40 km AURORA 45 km NEWMARKET 88 km BARRIE 125 km ORILLIA 148 km GRAVENHURST 194 km BRACEBRIGE 213 km HUNTSVILLE 337 km NORTH BAY 653 km IROQUOIS FALLS 712 km COCHRANE 830 km KAPUSKASING 927 km HEARST 1444 km THUNDER BAY 1896 km RAINY RIVER YONGE STREET IS THE LONGEST STREET IN THE WORLD.

The claim had earned Yonge Street a place in the 1978 *Guinness Book of World Records*: "The longest designated street in the world is Yonge Street, which runs north and west from Toronto, Canada. The first stretch, completed on February 16, 1796, ran 34 ½ miles. Its official length, now extended to Rainy River at the Manitoba-Minnesota border, is 1,178 miles." But, as the great pianist Glenn Gould said when he narrated a TV program about Toronto the year the *Trillium* collided with the *Normac*, Yonge Street "doesn't exactly end; it just sort of dissolves into the Ontario highway system…"

In May 1995 the city sent Captain John a surprising letter. A handsome dignified sign would be erected to identify what was styled "Captain John's Pier." A few months later, at a luncheon marking the Captain's twenty-fifth anniversary as a waterfront restaurateur, Chris Korwin-Kuczynski presented him with a framed certificate terming his ship as a "well-known landmark in our city." A hundred notables representing City Hall, the Harbour Commission, and the faithful *Toronto Star* observed the ceremony. On his naval blazer, the Captain wore a gold boat tie pin.

Some of the Captain's diners and closest friends had been ex-Yugoslavs. Steve Stavro, the Macedonian-born founder of the Knob Hill supermarket chain and sometime part-owner of the Toronto Maple Leafs. The ebullient globe-ranging *Toronto Star* photographer Boris Spremo, who arrived from Serbia as a 22-year-old the same year as Captain John, had, the *Star* reported, "stepped off the train at Union Station in 1957, with 14 bucks in his pocket, a Vespa scooter, a dream and two word of English – 'Okay' and 'Darling.'" George Chuvalo, the heavyweight boxer born of Croatian parents, certainly not known for his speed but for his preternatural endurance and granite chin: though often losing, he'd never been knocked down, twice vertically surviving 15 rounds with Muhammad Ali.

For many years, Captain John met for Saturday breakfast with friends at the Sweet Gallery in Etobicoke, initially known as the Steve Stavro Breakfast Club. Stavro (who died in 2006) was one of them, as was Chuvalo; George Gross, the Czech-born, long-time sports journalist for the *Toronto Sun* (who died the same year as Gross); and Hazel McCallion ("Hurricane Hazel.") The appellation for the perennial mayor of Mississauga, apparently immortal, alluded not to the destructive powers of the original Hurricane Hazel, which in 1954 pounded the Toronto area, washed out bridges and streets, killed 81 people, and made thousands homeless.

Rather, it referred to her unstoppable efforts to move the Mississauga skyline upward and onward. In the mid-1990s, she and several business-seeking Toronto-area Slovenian Canadians, including the Captain's old friend Frank Paznar, had travelled to Slovenia. Captain John's brother Anton met and hosted them at their sister Antonia's home in Lenart.

After the Second World War, many Slovenes had dispersed to the United States, Australia, Argentina – and Canada. In Canada, they had generally worked themselves into the upwardly mobile middle class. Surveys reported that a typical Slovene family consisted of a father, mother, and three children; one study found that 90 per cent of Slovenes lived in their own houses. After John Holer came to Canada in the late 1950s, he founded the Marineland amusement park, including areas to view dolphins, sea lions, killer whales, and belugas, and rides such as a roller coaster that looped across 30 acres. He became a close family friend of the Captain, who would drop by Marineland on his trips to Niagara Falls. Another celebrity was the accordion-playing Walter Ostanek, son of Slovene immigrants, who won three consecutive Grammy awards. By 1994, Slovenian Canadians could watch on TV one of their own, Elvis Stojko, whose mother was Hungarian but whose father was Slovene. The world figure-skating champion had dined at Captain John's with his wife and friends.

In 1993, one of the first sights that Dragana Varagic, an award-winning actress during her career with the National Theatre of Belgrade, saw when she arrived in Canada was the *Jadran* at the foot of Yonge Street. In 2007, now the Artistic Director of April Productions, she returned to it to star in *Have I None*, the British playwright Edward Bond's vision of a dystopian future set in 2077. She got the idea of staging and starring in it, not in the *Jadran*'s easeful main-deck dining room but in its dank lower interior. "Why not?" Captain John told her. Reckoning that the audience might buy drinks, or even dinner, he didn't charge her for the space. Larry Zappia, the play's director, quipped, "Hopefully the audience won't get seasick." They didn't. Gathering on the upper deck, they were led down narrow steps into the hold, an environment of cracked portholes, echoing acoustics, and bare light bulbs strung from the ceiling. Zappia described it as "rusty and rustic." All the better to depict a time in which family ties were abolished in the interests of public order.

♦ ♦ ♦

The 1970s were good years for the hospitality industry as people unleashed their wallets in hotels and restaurants. Captain John shared in the bounty: the *Normac* and the *Jadran* operated at a profit. The 1980s might have been almost as good for him, had not the *Trillium* rammed the *Normac* in 1981, followed by seven painful years of expensive litigation. But the decade had ended on a triumphant note when the Federal Court of Appeal upheld his claim against the municipality of Toronto. He had been encouraged to launch a restaurant in Cleveland aboard the *Normac* in 1989, and to embark on real estate speculations with Jeannine Sullivan.

His timing could not have been worse. The North American economy caught the flu in 1991-92 with the usual symptoms: slower economic growth, big government deficits, higher unemployment, collapsing real estate prices — all in all, less money to go around. Business was as bad in Cleveland as it was in Toronto. Near the end of 1991 Captain John shut down the Cleveland outpost, later selling the *Normac* to Nino Donatelli, a developer from Port Dalhousie near St.

Catharines, a port last seen by the *Normac* in 1969 when it had navigated the Welland Canal en route to Toronto. The Captain estimated he had sunk more than $1 million into the hard-luck ship. He sold it for $150,000, payments spread over five years. He and Sullivan sold the Cleveland house at a loss. Except for a farm in the name of Ivanka and her husband — which they retained, but later sold — the properties they had bought were foreclosed.

By this time, the Captain's and Sullivan's previous marriages had ended, and no religious prohibitions prevented them from getting wed in a Catholic church. But, whether they lived in Cleveland or Toronto singly or apart, they had begun to have strenuous business disagreements. As far as business was concerned, the Captain thought that Sullivan was spending more than she was making. By March 1992 their relationship, both romantic and financial, ended.

Sullivan, however, was in no doubt that she and the Captain had been married. In the aftermath of their parting, she believed that she was entitled to a share of his assets. In 1994 she launched an action in the Ontario Unified Family Court, claiming that they'd had an "intimate personal relationship" for almost 22 years, at least seven of which they had lived as common-law spouses. Captain John's lawyer argued that they hadn't lived together continuously.

In his judgment of June 22, Justice Thomas A. Beckett noted that the applicant was "one of those people who rarely throws away a greeting card." Sullivan's lawyer entered into evidence numerous fondly sentimental cards that the Captain had sent — as well as a ring he had given her. Much testimony centred on how much time she had spent on or off ships in Toronto and Cleveland. The Captain's lawyer argued that one period during which she was not aboard — May until

December 1990 – broke the continuity of couplehood. Despite the likeness of their names, Thomas A. Beckett bore scant resemblance to Thomas à Becket, the English saint and martyr. Captain John might have been forgiven in supposing that *he*, if not a saint, was at least a martyr. Justice Beckett didn't think so. He stated that, "Whether couples are separated is a question of intent, not geography; at least one of the parties must intend to permanently sever the relationship."

"Within the meaning of the Family Law Act, Sullivan and the Captain had been spouses," the judge concluded. Other Family Court issues, i.e., money, remained to be settled.

In June 2001, Andre Mayer of *Toronto Life* magazine reported on the all-season Christmas lights draped across the *Jadran*'s upper deck, the red-carpeted gang-plank, and the wooden likeness of the Captain standing on Queens Quay West, creating what he called a "fabulously kitschy" effect. The Captain, Mayer observed, wore "the same mutton chops that greeted customers on opening day 31 years ago, and when playing maitre d' or presiding over banquets and wedding parties, he dons the same tacky captain's uniform: a crested double-breasted jacket (cuffs banded with gold stripes), white pants and white shoes." You could, he said, "be quietly enjoying your rainbow trout meunière, only to be startled by a curious sucking noise and look up to find Letnik behind the bar – flashlight and tool kit in hand – personally fixing the soda dispenser."

For the new year of 2002, the *Toronto Star* canvassed notables on their resolutions. "For some, with 9/11 in mind," it said, "this will be a year to enjoy the good things in life, to treat people better, to be more tolerant, to not sweat the small stuff. For others the vows are more mundane: more exercise, less procrastination, to savour more fine wines..." Captain John's was simplest of all: "My resolution is that it is a pleasure to work. I enjoy what I'm doing, and I hope I can do it for another 32 years."

He was still doing it in 2010. That year the hundredth anniversary of the *Trillium*'s launching was celebrated at a dinner held aboard the *Jadran*. The city might have been unaware of the irony of celebrating there a vessel that had rammed and indirectly sank the Captain's other ship, but the Captain was aware of it. He was not one to bear grudges, though. Business was business.

Jeannine Sullivan had been an unsecured creditor of the Captain's company on the basis of a loan she had made during the period of their involvement. There were secured creditors, too, notably the Duca Credit Union, to whom after 1998 the Captain owed about $395,000 on a fixed loan and $120,000 on a line of credit. The following year Sullivan got a court order that awarded her 50 per cent of the shares in the Captain's company, subject to the prior pledge to Duca. Now remarried and living in Hamilton, she assigned the shares to her new husband's numbered company, which in January 2002 moved for seizure and sale of the shares committed to Duca. But of course the great question was whether the Captain's company had *any* net assets.

In February, the Captain sought bankruptcy protection. Under the proposal he filed, secured creditors like Duca would be paid according to arrangements they presently had with his company or ones they mutually agreed to. The Captain only employed 10 people, compared to dozens previously, and his debts were massive. He sought to sell the business and assets to an incorporated company. The proposal stated that Captain Normac's Riverboat Inn Ltd. owed secured creditors $200,000 and unsecured creditors $3.4 million, including restaurant suppliers and an old family friend in Slovenia. He proposed to fully repay unsecured creditors owed less than $5,000; most larger unsecured creditors would get $15,000 right away, with another $15,000 to follow in 12 months.

In March his creditors scheduled a meeting to vote on the repayment plan. Having learned of the meeting, Jeannine Sullivan called his bid for bankruptcy protection an attempt "to flush me out as 50 per cent-owner." She added, "The company is being flipped and the assets flipped out." She disputed an appraisal valuing the ship, the company's main asset, at $200,000. Sure that her claim as an unsecured creditor would not get fairly dealt with, she rushed to get the meeting postponed. Justice Maurice Cullity of the Ontario Superior Court ruled that "no resolutions or decisions made at the meeting of creditors are to be implemented" until he could meet with both sides.

In June, Justice Cullity stayed the bankruptcy go-ahead pending a hearing on whether the Captain's company was solvent. In October, Justice Donald Cameron of the Ontario Superior Court of Justice heard the case of Sullivan v. Letnik. For some months, Duca had contemplated selling the shares the Captain had pledged to it, and now Sullivan and her mother Julia Jamroz aimed to block what they considered a rushed sale to a single buyer. She maintained that, although she could not purchase the business she had given Captain John and Duca the names of four possible buyers who were in the restaurant business.

Justice Cameron could not make much sense of the company books, but he noted that the Captain had paid down the municipal taxes by $23,000 in 2002 and had part of the *Jadran*'s hull painted that spring. This made the Justice think that the company was turning a profit. Overall, he found that the Captain owed Duca $515,000 secured by his assets; he owed Sullivan $295,000 in unsecured debt, and Jamroz $55,000. Captain John testified that articles in the press in the spring publicized his financial problems, adversely affecting the business; if Duca ran a for-sale advertisement he might just as well shut down the business. Duca concurred. Justice Cameron ruled that the "terms and conditions of the Duca proposal were not commercially reasonable; 13 days was not sufficient notice, and sufficient advertising of the bid process had not been carried out."

Duca did seek other buyers. In the event, the Captain had in mind a buyer of the Duca shares. This turned out to be his daughter Denise. Some of the debts, including more than $60,000 in unpaid taxes to the City of Toronto, would be transferred to the new owner, who would hire the Captain to manage the restaurant. A numbered company proved to be as convenient to Captain John it had been to Jeannine Sullivan: one owned by his daughter Denise, who had completed four years in Business and Administration at Seneca College, acquired Captain Normac's Riverboat Inn Ltd. The Captain declared personal bankruptcy. But he later recovered his company when Denise transferred it back to him. He and his ship were still afloat.

In 2009, the *Jadran* and all it held was up for sale again. The price: $1.5 million, later slashed to $1.1 million. People came to look, but none stayed to bid. The ever-flexible Duca still held a mortgage. A more formidable obstacle was that any buyer was bound to a year-to-year mooring lease: at the Port Authority's pleasure it could be cancelled at any time. The buyer would also have to pay a monthly sum for the curbless cement "sidewalk" that ran the length of the *Jadran*'s berth. And, the old, old problem: Captain John's was taxed as property, not as a ship.

With Captain John's establishment for sale, the *Globe and Mail* asked a variety of individuals what could be done with it. A CBC-Radio host, Steven Sabados, thought it could be "a dinner and show experience called The Love Boat." Another radio host, Sook-Yin Lee, suggested "an adult playground. Keep the name and the nautical theme. Events could include shuffleboard competitions, tango lessons and night-time summer screenings of movies connected to water and sea life. Local artists could thematically decorate private sleeping cabins to rent out for overnight stays. You could suntan and drink martinis on the upper deck and the side of the ship could be converted into a climbing wall. If you fall off, you simply plunge into Lake Ontario." The proposal of David Crombie, the former mayor, was tamer: "Perhaps Waterfront Toronto could think of it as something they might want to use for an orientation centre for the waterfront. It would talk about the waterfront's past, present and future." The most inventive ideas came from hoteliers and restaurateurs. Christina Zeidler, president of the Gladstone Hotel, suggested it be called the Mariner Miller – a nod to Mayor David Miller. It would grow its own green roof. There could be a farmers' market and a fish market. Because we're trying to bring back the lake, there would be this whole focus on local, sustainable fishing. You could have a bar there called the Clean Water Bar. It would be all Toronto tap water, but it could be flavoured. It should have a speakeasy called the Dirty Water and it opens after the farmers' market shuts down. So the boat would be used during the day and at night. And you could get married in the Dirty Water Bar or the Clean Water Bar." The ambitious chef Marc Thuet "would do a cabaret like in Paris. Think of Folies Bergère. It would be a Cirque du Soleil/cabaret experience. Some nights I would do a nice supper club.... It's like eating dinner in the Titanic. Then, after a certain hour, it would turn into a dance club. You would have to gut the interior, but with a top designer you can do something really sexy." The idea of chef Mark McEwan, host of the Food Network's *The Heat* and owner of Bymark restaurant was the most succinct. "It would be fun to sink it and create a dive site to drive a new kind of tourism."

No one had thought of doing that with the *Normac.*

"I'm 72," the Captain told a newspaper reporter. I don't feel like it, but I am. It's time to sell." Asked where he'd move if the vessel was sold, he said, "Maybe the new guy might need me." As he said so often before, "The restaurant is really my life, my hobby and my business." To another reporter, he said, "The boat needs a little bit of upgrading. And it needs younger blood. More than half the ship is still empty. There is a lot of potential here for a young person," he said. "They can make it into a hotel, a lounge, or even a casino." Referring to the waterfront, he said, "We need more attraction down here." He added, "It's not going to be an overnight sale. It's going to be a while to find a proper person. Because it's a ship, it's not a building. They have to know how to look after it."

PART THREE

THE CAPTAIN'S TABLE

Since the 1980s, all the aromatic crosscurrents of Toronto dining had passed the Captain by. Sustainable, organic meat, fish, and produce from southern Ontario that appealed to local food lovers. The blossoming of small ethnic restaurants from every corner of the earth. Fusion, vegan, pan-Asian cooking, and no cooking at all. The Food Channel on cable TV. The rise to superstar status of chefs like Jamie Kennedy, Michael Stadtlander, and Sasur Lee. All-you-can-eat sushi. Foodie trends left him unaffected. He did not serve his mother's Slovenian specialties. After all, his target clientele — tourists, banqueters, novelty-seekers — were largely uninterested in culinary exotica or in fine dining. A commercial motto held that "The customer is always right," though it was usually said in the same tone as a defeated electoral candidate might use in saying that the voters were always right. Gourmets could be discounted; what mattered to the Captain was that the seats got filled.

In November 1977, some seven years after the Captain opened his floating restaurant, the *Globe and Mail* summarized the findings of its reigning restaurant critic, Joanne Kates: "Your sense of balance feels a little strange from eating on a boat in the water, but kids will love the idea. The decor is, of course, boatish and the menu is, as is usual for such harbour restaurants mediocre seafood. It's very noisy, so no one will notice your kids, and they'll love charging up the gangplank."

Presumably Kates did not mean gangplank in the pirate sense, otherwise the kids would have dropped, wildly kicking, into Toronto Harbour.

A more sober assessment came from an anonymous person on *www.yelp.ca* in late March 2010. Although lukewarm about the food, he or she noted, "Captain John's has a very personal feel. This is probably because you can often see John Letnik seating tables or preparing drinks. At the end of the evening, I spotted John cleaning glasses. His distinguished face is impossible to miss, even if he has aged since the pictures in the ship were taken. I said hi and he was extremely welcoming. I also had to shamelessly get a picture with him." The reviewer closed, "Captain John's, because of its iconic place in Toronto's history, is an experience that ought to be, well experienced; even if you only go once."

In August 2008, the *Toronto Star*'s online portal *www.thestar.com* posted, "Where locals fear to tread," inviting comments on local landmarks, and asked, "Are tourists missing out on the real Toronto — or are we?" Deborah Dundas replied:

> Captain John's big boat has been at the pier at the bottom of Yonge Street as long as I can remember. The lustre has dimmed on its renown in this town, so I figured it was now or never to give it a visit.

> While I think it's a shadow of what it once was, the entrance is littered with Consumers' Choice Awards for every year in the past decade (including this year). So it's got a following.
>
> Truly, it's got a charm all its own. We stopped in for a coffee and a piece of pie - the coffee was fine and the lemon meringue was tart and fluffy, as it should be. The dining room on this Monday night was scattered with diners; a woman stopped to talk to two young couples out for dinner and give her recommendation: "I'm not much of a fish person but this was lovely."
>
> The fixtures are faded, the carpet needs changing, and it desperately needs to be aired out. But I'd be curious enough to go back and taste the chowder. If the smiles on the other diners are anything to go by, its old-fashioned charm still pleases.
>
> It's such a familiar landmark I'd miss it if it were gone. Please, though, Captain, would you update this boat?

In answer to Dundas's poignant question, Captain John perhaps would have updated the boat — if he could have afforded it.

Anna V. of Toronto in October 2008 also put in a good word for the Captain: "...the real reason you come to Captain John's is for the kitsch of eating on a giant ship on lake Ontario, let's be honest. So if you just want the novelty, go in the afternoon and have a beer on the back deck outside. And make sure you meet Captain John himself, he's a fantastic character..."

The fantastic character reacted with philosophic calm to any opprobrium directed his way. He had to take complains seriously, he knew, but it also seemed to him that some customers complained for the sheer joy of complaining. Among the thousands of them over the years there were bound to be critics.

If blogs are the ideal place for people to wildly express disapproval, guestbooks by their nature tend to accentuate the positive. Certainly, this was true of the *Jadran* guestbook the Captain maintained between June 14, 2009 and August 26, 2011. In 2010 alone, his guests signed compliments in Japanese, French, German, and Slovenian. True, Rana of Mississauga said, "Very Terrible Experience," and Resha of the same city wrote, "I'm very disappointed. I don't know where to begin."

On the other hand, the "Fam. Sofrenic" from Australia commented, "FANTASTIC" and Jackie Dennison of England said, "Fabulous Place. Great Service. Amazing food." Reg and Consuelo Klassan of Toronto noted that they'd been coming there for 25 years. On July 1, Jerry and Martin Agnew of Columbus, Indiana, reflected, "We were married and had our reception here 20 years ago July 22, 1989." Also nostalgic were "David & Alissya" of Vancouver, who observed on July 21: "Beautiful 15th Wedding Anniversary! (our last time here was when we got engaged 15 ½ years ago. Best Mahi Mahi ever! Thanks for the delicious cheesecake & candle!!!" Overseas visitors were impressed. Alex Boudet of France wrote, "It's a super good food. I loved it!" and from Mario Dedolf, Astrid Weser, and Tobias Weser of Germany: *"Danke, es war seher schön!"* The "Bridglal Family" of Trinidad and India sent a mixed message: "Great time, great service this place is fucking expensive!" From Russia, more or less with love, "FB" said flatly, "Was good meal."

♦ ♦ ♦

Like their Polish co-religionists to the north, the Roman Catholics of Slovenia had never been noted for philosemitism. So it was a little surprising that, here in Toronto, the Captain was attracted to the Jews in his midst. The Captain undoubtedly had a fellow feeling for them. One, an enduring friend, was a developer named Alex Beder, whom he had met at City Hall. Beder had dropped out of high school at 14 to help out in his father's fur business, becoming a fitness fanatic and inveterate writer of letters to newspaper editors, speaking up for Israel. In 1933, after a softball game in Christie Pits park, Beder had joined young Jews, Ukrainians, and Italians in battling the white supremacist Pits gang, a.k.a. the Swastika Club, a riot much bloodier than any following the average softball game.

In 1996, Beder got the idea of celebrating his ninetieth birthday by mounting a free meal for the homeless, enlisting Captain John, who was a regular guest at family Sabbath dinners and Passover Seders at the home of Beder's nephew Robert and his wife Sharon. Since the homeless the Captain and Alex Beder had in mind numbered about a thousand people, and their event would cost about $10,000, it was no small undertaking. Donors and sponsors were rounded up, drawn from the Captain's acquaintances and business contacts: his old friend Steve Stavro, the Knob Hill Farms grocery mogul; his banker the Duca Credit Union; his food broker Mike Shasky — Shasky and his wife Mary later presented him with a metal model ship that helped decorate the *Jadran*'s dining room. The Salvation Army supplied many of the homeless, and lent helping hands to serve them, aided by police volunteers.

At the first meal, Beder said, "I'm very happy to be here. At my age I'm happy to be anywhere." The chicken or turkey dinners, the first one held on the United Nations international day for the eradication of poverty, became an annual event. Beder died in 2004 at the age of 97 in Sunnybrook Hospital, with the Captain among those at his side.

The Captain, who called the event "homeless feeding," formally named "Feed the Hungry," kept the tradition going. Usually at the end of the first week in October or November, there were four sittings of 200 to 300 lining up at a simple buffet, typically of onion soup or Manhattan clam chowder; salmon fillet or chicken; choice of potato, rice, and vegetables; bread and butter; choice of coffee, tea, or a soft drink; a piece of cake, mixed fruit cocktail, and cookies. At the end of the feast, the Salvation Army gave out donated gloves, socks, and blankets.

The homeless were not the only object of the Captain's benefactions. Mixed in with the politicians and celebrities on the walls of the Captain's ship were framed certificates, testimonials, and thank-you letters. The Captain tended to favour police causes. A certificate of appreciation from the Ontario Handgun Association, Police Revolver Clubs of Ontario, for contributions to 1990 Ontario Provincial Championship for Police Pistol Combat. Thanks from the Metropolitan Toronto Police Hold-Up Squad to Member No. 006 (the Captain's wallet held his membership card, dated 1990 and signed by Det. Insp. Bill Bolton.) Thanks for a donation to the Kitchener RCMP Annual Golf Tournament. A certificate from Alexandra Park Community "for generous and continuing support towards our Alexandra Park Remembrance Appreciation Day." Thanks from the Heart & Stroke Federation of Canada, the Greenbank Assistance Program (about a lunch for Food Bank clients), the

Martin Grove United Church, and the Good Shepherd Ministries. Appreciation for contributing to the Canadian Yugoslav Cultural Association and Nikola Tesla School, and a Citizen's Award from the Federal Republic of Yugoslavia on the occasion of his fiftieth birthday.

For many centuries, Jews had been an unmistakable presence in the Captain's native region. For example, they lived for centuries in Maribor, the city close to where the Lettniggs or Letniks lived in St. Ana and Lenart. As early as 1103, one "David son of Moses" was mentioned in Ptuj, few kilometres away and the oldest town in Slovenia. Maribor was important to Jews in medieval times, who worshipped at an impressive synagogue. Until the late fifteenth century Jews prospered as artisans, bankers, moneylenders, and merchants, but this relative prosperity came to an end when the Austrian Emperor, Maximilian I, expelled all the Jews of Styria, including Maribor. The synagogue became All Saints church. After the Second World War and the Holocaust, it should have come as no surprise that by the twenty-first century there were only a few hundred observant Jews left in Slovenia and, in Ljubljana, merely one synagogue.

On one of his trips to Slovenia in the mid-1980s, the Captain had paid a visit to his cousin Franc, who was dying of cancer. Franc showed him a piece in a Croatian newspaper about a Jewish professor of mathematics in Kiev named Dmitri Letnik, accompanied by a photograph of him riding a bicycle for which he'd designed a sail affixed to the front wheel. The piece mentioned that Dmitri's grandfather had fought in the Austro-Hungarian army on the Eastern Front during the First World War before he was captured. Since Letnik is an uncommon name, especially in Ukraine, Franc had wondered if he might be the same person as his uncle, who had been a prisoner of war in Tashkent. Tashkent in Central Asia, the capital of Uzbekistan, was a long way from Kiev, but still.

Intrigued, Franc had written in Russian and English to Dmitri in Kiev, but got no reply. Then a letter arrived from Haifa. Dmitri, whose father had been a doctor and a general in the Russian army, had immigrated to Israel, a move that had brought with it some peril. His father, his wife, and a son had flown there while he and another son sailed there on a yacht. A ship had struck the yacht, sinking it. The rescued father and son had lost everything but their lives.

Dmitri was as interested in family roots as Franc and the Captain. The Captain was soon corresponding with him, and they even spoke on the phone. In 2007, Dmitri visited Canada. When he turned up at the *Jadran*, the Captain recognized a family resemblance before they even spoke.

The Captain knew that in 1735 the family had changed its name to Letnik from the Yiddish-sounding Lettnigg. So was the Captain Jewish, however remotely? It was possible. Whether or not he was grasping at straws in supposing a Jewish ancestry for himself, the Captain vowed that on his next trip to Slovenia he would travel to Israel. He would get a DNA blood test to really find out if he and Dmitri Letnik were related.

Alex Beder had been a keen supporter of the Association for the Soldiers of Israel, the Canadian partner of the Association for the Wellbeing of Israel's Soldiers, (AWIS), whose predecessor had been founded by David Ben-Gurion to provide blankets and other comforts for Jews fighting in the British Army during World War Two. It was the only Canadian non-profit organization in Canada devoted to the wellbeing of Israeli soldiers on active duty. Its money went to found mobile clubrooms, fitness rooms, and synagogues on Israeli Defence Force bases to, as its website said, "ease the burden faced by young soldiers defending the Jewish homeland." The Captain helped to ease the burden by buying tickets to its fund-raising galas. Although he was not one to volunteer opinions about the territorial politics of the fought-over Middle East, he admired the way the Association helped soldiers.

This was not the only Jewish cause he supported in league with Alex Beder. From 1996, Holy Blossom Temple, Canada's largest Reform synagogue, was the first Jewish congregation to join a nondenominational coalition's "Out of the Cold" program to offer shelter, clothing, and meals to those in need. The Captain supplied salmon as well as seafood chowder. He was careful to leave out the clams.

CAPTAIN'S SLOVENIAN HERITAGE

The Captain was not homesick for Slovenia. He had left the country when he was young, and essentially grew up in Canada. He'd hardly cut himself off, though: monthly he received the magazine-like newspaper *Novice* (News) from Lenart, its population holding steady at about 2,600, compared to Maribor's 248,000. His mother, brother, and sisters from the Old Country had all come to visit. After the Balkan civil wars, the Captain had noticed that more ex-Yugoslavs (Serbs, Croats, Slovenes) had been travelling, including some from Lenart. He did not celebrate any special days of Slovenian significance – Independence Day, October 29, and the like – but he was directly responsible for some new Slovene Canadians: in the 1950s his wife Ana, in the 1960s his sister Ivanka, and in the 1980s his niece Daniela, who worked on the *Jadran* and, before she married, helped run the restaurant. From the late 1970s onward, he helped to organize Canada-Slovenia exchanges of entertainers and children's groups; a well-known ensemble, the Šavinska Oktet, had played on the *Jadran*.

His daughter Denise had been attending Havergal College, the elite girls' school founded in 1894 by Ellen Mary Knox, the unmarried daughter of an Anglican bishop and sister to the later-famous Roman Catholic apologist and Bible translator Ronald Knox and E. V. Knox, the long-time editor of *Punch*. Among other attainments, Denise was an accomplished figure skater. In 1984, the Captain took her to watch the triple salchows at the Winter Olympics in Sarajevo – and to visit the granite tombstone of her grandfather Janez Letnik in a Lenart cemetery. For his work on cultural exchanges and in raising funds to equip a children's ward in a Maribor hospital and present a scanner to a Ljubljana hospital the Captain got a birthday present in 1988: a Citizen's Award presented to him by the Yugoslavian consul. That same year, after getting assurances that his life would not be in danger, he was given a private tour of the Parliament Building and the Tito Museum in Belgrade.

Following World War Two, Josip Broz Tito had shaken off the iron clutch of Stalin and his Soviet successors to impose his own idiosyncratic brand of socialism in Yugoslavia. At first a pocket Stalinist, he eventually gave socialism a market face while binding under his rule an ostensibly ragtag, inward-looking band of nations. "We have solved the national question," he prematurely boasted in 1962. By the 1960s, he had industrialized the country, including Captain John's home district, Lower Styria, especially the city of Maribor. His limited version of a free market economy had made Croatia and Slovenia wealthier. Internationally, he allowed Yugoslavians to travel freely and to emigrate, and adroitly placed his country on neutral ground between the competing sides of the Cold War. Under his leadership, Yugoslavia became a founding member of the Non-Aligned Movement, in 1961 including

Egypt's Gamal Abdel Nasser, India's Jawaharlal Nehru, Indonesia's Sukarno and Ghana's Kwame Nkrumah, establishing strong ties with the Third World.

Up until 1980, Tito's political dictates and personal lifestyle (his love of hunting, home metalworking, dandyish uniforms, his daily four packs of cigarettes smoked in a holder, and his 32 official residences) had dominated Yugoslavia, even if for some years he had delegated everything other than key decisions to underlings. In 1979, he became ill from circulation problems in his legs, and one of them was amputated in early 1980 at a Ljubljana hospital. He died on May 4, aged 89. Attending his funeral were four kings, 31 presidents, six princes, and 22 prime ministers from 128 different countries.

After Tito's death, the Yugoslav economy was in tatters due to some of his fiscal policies. Politically, there was a power vacuum. Into the space created by both conditions rushed all the nascent forces of nationalism. A baby-faced former banker named Slobodan Milošević stoked the fears of the minuscule but vigorous Serbian minority in Kosovo, which many Serbs regarded as their spiritual heartland. Not only did Kosovo hold many of the most significant Orthodox monasteries, it had been the medieval core of the Serbian Empire. Moreover, the Battle of Kosovo in 1389 became the most important event in Serbia's national mythology. During the battle most of the combatants died, and both leaders, Serbia's Prince Lazar and the Ottoman Turks' Sultan Murad were killed, the latter by a Serb posing as a defector. It says something about the endemic Serbian sense of martyrdom that a military calamity became endlessly commemorated. In a 1987 speech near the battlefield, Milošević – during a period when both extremist Serbs and Albanians assassinated and kidnapped – declared that Serbs would never again be beaten.

In Croatia, the rabble-rousing Milošević had a baleful nationalist equivalent in its President, Franjo

Tudjman. In Bosnia, a patchwork quilt of Serbs, ethnic Muslims, and Croats made for a dysfunctional family, united only by their love of football. "Why did the war start in Croatia, not Bosnia?" went a dark joke. "Because Bosnia advanced directly to the finals." Slovenia, much more homogeneous in language and religion, was not immune to the havoc outside its borders that ensued after 1991 – to note two infamous examples, the Serbian and Bosnian Serb armies' militarily futile three-year siege of multiethnic Sarajevo, and the Bosnian Serbs' massacre of Muslim men and boys in Srebrenica – became determined to go its own way.

The roots of secession may have lain less with politics than with economics. Captain John thought so, anyway. Slovenia long had been the most prosperous Yugoslav republic. Slovenes, only eight per cent of the population, produced almost 25 per cent of all Yugoslav exports, and was generally considered to have the best roads, the most efficient factories, and the best tourist resorts. They bitterly resented its wealth being drained away to sustain an expensive, inefficient federal government.

The wider Yugoslav conflict began in the aftermath of a constitutional crisis. A new 1974 constitution had decentralized power, counting on Tito's authority to remain the binding agent. The federal government would handle foreign affairs, defence, internal security, and intergovernmental matters; everything else would devolve to the six constituent republics and two autonomous provinces. The result was the kind of situation that gives Balkanization a bad name. After Tito's death, decision-making at the top became paralyzed, and competing interests paramount. Croatia sought to secede from Yugoslavia; a large Serb minority sought to secede from Croatia. Croatia and Slovenia supported Albanian separatist aspirations in Kosovo, and in 1990 sought to devolve federal power further. Foiled at a hastily convened Congress of the League of Communists of Yugoslavia was convened, Croatia and Slovenia walked out. The all-Yugoslav Communist party collapsed just as, a year earlier, Communism had crumbled in nearly all the other Eastern European countries.

A substantial part of the Yugoslav military was still in the hands of Serbia, or at least the Serbians that Milošević claimed to represent. It went into action to defend compatriots in Croatia. On June 25, 1991, Slovenia and Croatia declared independence from what had now become the former Yugoslavia. What was still called the Yugoslav National Army attacked Slovenia in what became known as the Ten-Day War. Unlike what had happened in Croatia and had begun to happen in Bosnia and Herzegovina, it ended in a truce.

What was rapidly becoming the *former* Federal Republic of Yugoslavia went from bad to worse. In 1991, a mostly Serb-populated region of Croatia called Krajina declared its own independence, which naturally led to internal strife. In 1995, with U.S. support, Croatia drove more than 200,000 Serbs out of the country, mainly to Serbia. The expulsion was underreported; not so, NATO's air strikes against the Bosnian Serbs the same year, which led to the U.S.-sponsored Dayton Accord in November. The Accord divided the former Bosnia into the strangely tripartite Federation of Croats and Bosniaks (Bosnian Muslims) and the Serb-dominated Republika Srbska.

Tito had done his Machiavellian best to keep Kosovo's majority ethnic Albanians and minority Serbs in political balance. A belated effect of the Croatian and Bosnian war was NATO's bombing of Serbia in the spring of 1999, ostensibly a reaction against Serbian persecution of Kosovars in a region where the separatist Kosovo Liberation Army had long been active. NATO's bombloads may have been fuelled by the West's sense that its inaction – not to mention the UN's pitiful peacekeeping efforts – had prolonged the carnage in Bosnia. After heavy bombing began, hundreds of thousands of Kosovars fled into Macedonia, their exodus perhaps due as much to NATO's wayward bombs as to Serbian persecution. NATO's attacks, in which Canada took part, had its embarrassments – the Serbs downed a Stealth bomber, and a NATO bomb inadvertently hit the Chinese Embassy in Belgrade – and was punctuated by pointless destruction of a farmers' market in Nis and a graceful Danubian bridge in Novi Sad. But NATO's inevitable triumph also led to the downfall of Serbia's quasi-genocidal leader, Slobodan Milošević.

Back in 1991, the loss of the Yugoslav market severely strained Slovenia's industry, and unemployment rocketed. But the economy largely recovered. In 1993 Slovenia opened an embassy in Ottawa, and in 2004 it entered the European Union, the same year the United Nations granted it a seat. Like many European nations, not to mention Canada and the United States, population growth was slowing and more young adults lived with their parents. Along with diplomatic gains, the same people lived in the country and the same national stereotypes persisted, even in a Slovenian government website of 2006: "Generally, Slovenes describe themselves as industrious, honest, a bit jealous, good singers who enjoy a good glass of wine, perhaps a bit on the melancholic side and with a slight propensity for extremism." Slovenes were still honest, calm, reserved, disciplined, conscientious, and hardworking. "In this respect we are similar to the Germans, yet distinct in one important characteristic – Germans have an essential sense of community and collectivism while Slovenes are much more individualistic in our industriousness." Rather candidly, the website also noted that Slovenes were "marked with another characteristic, that of self-destructiveness. Experts see the latter as a result of a combination of aggressiveness and introversion. This can be seen in the large number of suicides, alcoholism, and traffic accidents." Slovenes were still great skiers and alpinists, though.

In 2007, about 30 years after Ivan Letnik had crossed the boundary, all border controls between Slovenia and Austria ended. Ten years earlier, Canada's recognition of Slovenia had a minor repercussion in the ongoing battle between federal and Quebec separatist forces. In 1997, Bernard Landry, the Quebec Deputy Premier, had likened Slovenian secession to what he hoped would be Quebec's. The Canadian Slovenian Congress wrote him a stiff letter, copied to the Prime Minister, Jean Chrétien, and the Intergovernmental Affairs Minister, Stéphane Dion, denying any analogy. Offering an abridged history of the Yugoslav breakup, the Congress said Landry's statement was "absurd." In the ninth century, Slovenes had democratically elected their dukes in Carinthia (present-day Slovenia) and Thomas Jefferson had been inspired by this precedent in writing Americans' Declaration of Independence. But the Yugoslav constitution had affirmed each republic's right to self-determination, the Congress noted: "Slovenian independence and international recognition cannot be used as an example nor as a model for Quebec separation."

Born a pan-Yugoslavian, Captain John had always tried to keep himself apart from nationalist politics and racial retaliation. Although he donated to the electoral campaigns of candidates on the conservative side of the Canadian political spectrum, he could not, as a prudent restaurateur, bar anyone from his door, rather like a convenience-store proprietor who allows competing political parties to affix their posters to his front window. Nor by prudence or instinct, did he pick sides in the civil wars that were raging in his homeland. He did, however, view Slobodan Milošević's ambitions for a Greater Serbia to be a lesser, latter-day parallel to Hitler's vision of a transcontinental Reich. In any case, fistfights between Serbs and Croats did not break out inside his precincts.

During the Second World War, the Captain's fellow Yugoslav Canadians had suffered twin anxieties. Some of them served in the Canadian armed forces, or had sons or daughters who did; all were anguished about the fate of their families or close friends back home. After the war, some clung to their tribal Partisan or conservative Catholic loyalties (for a time there was a Toronto branch of the Slovenian Home Guard) some felt themselves part of the emerging Titoist Yugoslavia. Although proudly Slovenian, Captain John had belonged in, and in a sense belonged to, Yugoslavia. In any case, the Canadian national idea – some might say an illusion – was that newcomers would forsake their old-country allegiances and enmities while adding multicultural colours to their new flag.

THE CITY AND THE LAKE

In the years since Captain John had first docked the *Normac* in Toronto in 1969 the city had come of age. But what age?

Middle age, perhaps, but with adolescent twinges of envious resentment. In a 1987 interview, the polymathic actor and writer Peter Ustinov said, "Toronto is a kind of New York operated by the Swiss." Toronto's envious aspiration to become a simulated New York, that most and least American of cities, was succeeded by the aspiration to become a "world city." This at least was an advance on its little envy of Manhattan, or its shame at not having developed a waterfront in the exemplary way that Chicago had. Up to then, Toronto had traded on its status as a generically interchangeable North American city for market-testing or film-making purposes — movies set in U.S. cities had been shot there, among them *American Psycho, Chicago, Good Will Hunting,* and *Police Academy.*

Apart from the self-aggrandizing hype, or its cinematographically convenient anonymity, there was some evidence for Toronto's ascent to world status. In the early years of the twenty-first century the tide of British and European newcomers had not exactly gone out, but a new tide had come in: Ghanaians and Somalis from Africa; Koreans, Indians, Pakistanis, and Iranians from Asia; Jamaicans and Trinidadians from the West Indies. More Spanish was heard on public transit. Chinese had lived in Canada since pre-Confederation days, indeed had helped to build the Canadian Pacific Railway. Like Blacks, they had often suffered under systemic bigotry, especially in the first few decades of the twentieth century. Now, in the Greater Toronto Area, there were several distinct Chinatowns, many of their shopkeepers or restaurateurs emigrants from Hong Kong.

On subway cars it became obvious by sight and sound that most passengers likely hadn't been born in Canada, or hadn't spoken English as a first language. Viciously racist slurs of the Paki-joke type were no longer heard, even in impolite adult society. The tenor of Toronto society had radically changed since the Edwardian years when Dr. Ernest Jones, Sigmund Freud's advance man, had lived there, and wrote Freud that Torontonians were "a despicable race, exceedingly bourgeois, quite uncultured, very rude, very stupid and very narrow and pious." He could not have guessed that such an annual public ritual as the Santa Claus Parade – long sponsored by the T. Eaton Company, it had been the traditional November kickstart to Christmas shopping – would be replaced or vastly outscaled by the phantasmagorias of the Trinidad Carnival-inspired Caribana or by the culminating parade of Gay Pride Week, which drew as many as 100,000 watchers. Such nation-wide institutions as the Simpson's and Eaton's department-store chains, the latter ineptly stewarded by Timothy Eaton's great-grandsons, collapsed and were bought out. Where once Toronto had named its highways and public spaces after living politicians (Nathan Philips Square, Mel Lastman Square, the Gardiner Expressway) it now was more inclined to name swatches of greenery called parkettes after the locally famed (poets like George Faludy and Gwendolyn MacEwen, and the entrepreneur Ed Mirvish and his wife Anne.)

Influenced by the ideas of the urban thinker Jane Jacobs, Toronto had become aware of the importance of neighbourhoods, especially ones identifiable as ethnic, and this became reflected in real estate listings, street signage, the names of Business Improvement Associations, and just by word-of-mouth: Koreatown on Bloor Street from Honest's Ed west to Christie Street; Little India on Gerrard Street east of Coxwell Avenue. By now Little Italy had become progressively less Italian and more Portuguese; the real Little Italy was the Corso Italia on St. Clair Avenue West from Dufferin Street westward. The fulcrum of the downtown Chinatown remained the corner of Dundas Street and Spadina Avenue.

On an official Toronto city website map, Captain John's location was to be found as a slipper-shaped segment vaguely identified as "Waterfront Communities – The Island." In the mid-1950s, the new Metropolitan Toronto Council had tried to eject the islands' house and cottage leaseholders, aiming to replace their neighbourhood with recreational parkland on the mainland that had been robbed by newly built Gardiner Expressway. Fiercely attached to their homes, the islanders resisted, fighting legal and legislative battles. Although many homes had been demolished, the islanders gained a measure of victory in 1993, when the Ontario Government passed an act enabling them to purchase long-term leases.

Across from the islands, the central cityscape had markedly changed, and one big change had been averted: venerable Union Station had been saved from threatened demolition. North and slightly east of the Captain's ship, the St. Lawrence Market area, below the waterline when the town of York was founded in 1793, had sank into industrial decrepitude by the 1960s. But in the 1970s, with David Crombie now mayor, it had been revived as a residential neighbourhood centred on what had been City Hall, now a retail vendors' market. The Eaton Centre itself, which went up in 1977 and was one of the first downtown shopping malls in North America, largely presented a blank wall between Queen Street and Dundas Street, all the better to direct hordes of shoppers into its multilevelled atrium cum galleria. After 2002, opposite the Centre's main entrance, the new Dundas Square was a large nondescript wedge of cement, whose environs became half wannabe Times Square, half neon Tokyo. More than 100,000 pedestrians used the junction daily. On the 13 acres where Gooderham and Worts had once made booze, the Distillery District of cafés, restaurants, and shops opened, said to be the largest collection of Victorian-era industrial architecture in North America. Nothing like any of these developments occurred at the corner of Yonge Street and Queen's Quay West.

Nationally, Canada had also altered. The Canadians who thought that Indians lived in bands now had to reckon with the fact that they belonged to multiple Nations, and learned to style them First Peoples. In Quebec, the creation of another nation of quite a different kind, had been narrowly averted in a 1980 provincial referendum. The exploitation of natural resources, particularly petroleum, natural gas, and hydropower, had shifted wealth away from the factories and automotive plants of Quebec and Ontario, traditionally and geographically misleadingly termed "Central Canada," and toward Western Canada and, to a less transformative extent, the Atlantic Provinces.

Toronto had rudely displaced Montreal as a cultural capital and economic engine.

In tandem with these alterations in the economic landscape, national political parties had formed and reformed. The Bloc Québécois, the federal counterpart of the provincial Bloc Québécois, won their first seats in 1993. Out of the West, the populist Reform Party entered Parliament, and bonded with disaffected Progressive Conservatives to form the Canadian Alliance; in 2003, the Alliance merged with the PCs to form one Conservative Party.

The framed photos on the wall of the *Jadran*'s corridor also framed history – national, provincial, local – of the past 40 years. Prime ministers like the oleaginous Brian Mulroney ("the Jaw that walks and talks like a man," in the journalist Allan Fotheringham's memorable phrase); Jean Chrétien who, unscripted, was largely unintelligible in both French and English; and the blandly authoritarian Stephen Harper, had gone and come. Here on a corridor wall was a photo of Mulroney, prime minister 1984-93, with his wife Mila *née* Milica Pivnicki in Sarajevo. Her Bosnian Serb father, a psychiatrist, had immigrated to Canada to take up a research fellowship in Montreal the year before Captain John arrived in Quebec City. When she and her husband boarded the *Jadran,* the Captain was able to chat with her in Serbo-Croat.

Bill Davis ("Brampton Billy"), Ontario premier 1971-85, had also been a customer. Here on the wall was a photo of Davis's fellow premier, David Peterson, elected the year Davis had retired, with his blonde wife Shelley Peterson, actress and writer. Here was a group photo of the Captain, his old friend Steve Stavro, John Honderich, and Mel Lastman. The tall, bow-tied Honderich had been Editor of the *Toronto Star* before succeeding his father Beland as Publisher in 1994, before he resigned a decade later. Mel Lastman, founder of the Bad Boy Furniture chain, had been the decades-long mayor of North York, responsible for the Yonge strip of high-rise buildings between Sheppard Avenue and the North York Civic Centre, naming Mel Lastman Square after himself. He was Mayor of amalgamated Toronto from 1998 to 2003. In 1999, Lastman, who had once travelled to the Arctic to "sell a refrigerator to an Eskimo," called in the Canadian Army to remove snow after a blizzard – to nation-wide derision. In June 2001, prior to a trip to Mombasa, Kenya to support Toronto's bid for the 2008 Summer Olympics, he joked, "I just see myself in a pot of boiling water with all these natives dancing around me." Toronto did not win the bid.

Here also was a big photo of David Crombie, unveiling the sign designating Captain John's Pier. After his days as a 1960s political science teacher at Ryerson Institute of Technology he had become a politician himself. An urban-planning disciple of Jane Jacobs and enemy of expressways, the diminutive Crombie was from 1972 to 1978 hugely popular (the media called him "the tiny perfect mayor.") A photo of the dully well-intentioned and ineffectual David Miller, whose two-term mayoral regime Captain John abhorred, was not to be found, nor as yet was there one of Rob Ford, the 330-pound-plus Councillor from Etobicoke who was elected to City Hall in 2010 on a promise to cut the budgetary fat, seconded by his Etobicoke-Councillor, slightly less adipose brother, Doug Ford, Jr. The Fords liked buses, cars, and subways; they did not like bicycles and streetcars, especially when the latter, on streets or underground, were called light rapid transit. Across from the ferry docks a couple of blocks west of Captain John's, in fact, streetcars a.k.a. the LRT, surfaced or sank into tunnels connecting with Union Station.

The Captain had voted for Rob Ford. If it had been up to the improvident David Miller, he thought, he would have been put out of business five years earlier. He much preferred the pay-as-you-go policies of his old breakfast companion Hazel McCallion in Mississauga. In any case, it was sometimes just as well that Toronto's mayor represented more symbolic leadership than practical power: any mayor had to deal with a fractious Council.

♦ ♦ ♦

With the Don Valley Parkway, the oft-repaired and rebuilt Gardiner Expressway was one of two funnels that emptied a rush-hour torrent of people and traffic into central Toronto. A structure of surpassing ugliness, the Gardiner began in the western suburbs, skirted Lake Ontario from the junction of Highway 427 and the Queen Elizabeth Way, bypassed the Parkdale neighbourhood and the grounds of the Canadian National Exhibition, squatted atop massive concrete pillars for the part of its journey above Lake Shore Boulevard east of Bathurst Street, and abruptly ended where the north-south Don Valley Parkway did, just past the mouth of the Don River. Mingled with rising and falling views of the cityscape along its route, the Gardiner offered motorists blandishments from rooftop billboards, neon signs, and video boards, along with logos formed by planted yew bushes. On occasion the homeless located themselves in the dank shelter of its elevated ramps.

Whether Toronto would be crisscrossed by expressways became the paramount question surrounding construction of the Spadina Expressway, the great municipal *cause célèbre* of the late 1960s and early 1970s. To many, the proposed expressway was like a shot aimed at the city's heart, slicing southward from Eglinton Avenue to the waterfront. With the baleful example of the Gardiner in mind – not to mention their property values – residents, frequenters, and shop-owners in such venerable neighbourhoods as well-heeled Forest Hill, the gentrified, university-connected Annex, as well as such Spadina Avenue ethnic redoubts as Kensington Market and Chinatown, feared imminent uprooting.

In the forefront of the "Stop Spadina" movement was a newcomer, Jane Jacobs, an Annex resident and former American urban activist. She had fought Robert Moses, the emperor of expressways in New York City. The author of the enormously influential *The Death and Life of Great American Cities* (1961), Jacobs maintained that expressways killed neighbourhoods and downtown cores. Like George Orwell, she was one of those thinkers whose ideas could be appropriated by both Left and Right on the political spectrum. She deplored U.S. involvement in the Vietnam War, one of the reasons she had moved to Canada; she espoused citizen-level democracy; she opposed suburban sprawl and forms of capitalism that destroyed dense, mixed-use neighbourhoods. Yet she reserved her greatest scorn for the slum-clearance and high-rise public housing projects of big government. In her book *Systems of Survival: A Dialogue on the Moral Foundations of Commerce and Politics* (1992), she maintained that two patterns of moral behaviour obtained, the "commercial" and the "guardian." In her view, they should not be confused. The commercial syndrome applied to business owners, scientists, farmers, traders, charities, hunter-gatherers, and religious institutions. In modern society, each should have its proper domain.

In the battle against the Spadina Expressway, Jacobs and her allies prevailed. On June 3, 1971, Premier Bill Davis declared, "Cities were built for people and not cars. If we are building a transportation system to serve the automobile, the Spadina Expressway would be a good place to start. But if we are building a transportation system to serve people, the Spadina Expressway is a good place to stop."

The stoppage of Spadina had one consequence, as Robert Fulford points out in *Accidental City* (1995), "... comfortably antique neighbourhoods approximating the anti-Modernist visual ideal have survived downtown – at least in the minds of the aging urban professionals who took up the populist slogans of Stop Spadina, and occupied and gentrified the Victorian houses of Cabbagetown and the Annex. The massive internal migrations of well-heeled citizens during the astonishing real-estate boom of the 1980s, incidentally, did more to destroy the social fabric of 'traditional' neighbourhoods than the Spadina Expressway ever would have."

Fulford's contention was arguable, though it was certainly true that, as he says, Toronto "remains perhaps North America's only metropolis with expressways that abruptly stop, and empty their load onto ordinary streets – the Allen Road, as the Spadina Expressway is known today – and soaring ramps, like those at the eastern end of the Gardiner Expressway, that suddenly lose their surge, go limp and to the ground in the middle of nowhere."

Since it hugged the lakeshore, albeit from a height, the Gardiner was intrinsically connected to the vitality or otherwise of the Toronto waterfront. As Fulford says, "The Gardiner brought specialization to Toronto's lakeshore. For generations, the waterfront had been used for work, play, and, of course, transport: Lake Shore Boulevard ran along the water, and the railroad went into the harbour to connect with lake boats. These elements remained more or less in balance until the 1950s, but the Gardiner was built on a scale so overpowering that it made everything else marginal. It transformed an enormous part of the waterfront area into a transmission belt for cars."

It had "blocked off the Canadian National Exhibition (which has been in decline ever since), and cast a shadow over dozens of downtown streets. After the Gardiner went up, it continued to thwart some fairly ambitious attempts to use the lakefront for recreation. Ontario Place, the modernist pleasure park on the lake, has been a victim of the Gardiner ever since it opened in 1971; ironically, it's surrounded by transportation (the expressway and the railroad) but remains hard to reach."

The Gardiner had severed the Parkdale neighbourhood from its once-popular Sunnyside amusement park, then largely destroyed the latter. The Martin Goodman Trail pathway for joggers and cyclists, which the city had set up in the vicinity of the Humber River far to the west, was, Fulford says, was "darkened by what passes overhead."

Even when Fred Gardiner's wishes were thwarted, he exacted a belated revenge. Fort York, whose buildings dated from the War of 1812, inconvenienced his expressway and his first idea was simply to move it somewhere else. An outcry forced Gardiner to route his highway to the south of it. Today, Fulford says, "Fort York stands isolated in a lonely triangle formed by the railway, Bathurst Street, and the expressway." In sum,

> The Gardiner and the old railroad bridges together produce a forbidding atmosphere. To walk south on York from Front to Queen's Quay on the waterfront is to experience the automobile age at its most oppressive. You pick your way across a series of crossings, some of them made more dangerous by the

> fact of drivers coming down from the Gardiner, or going up to it, are preoccupied with negotiating the ramps. The Gardiner also destroyed southern Yonge Street, changing it from an urban street into an adjunct of the traffic system. Walking down Yonge to the *Toronto Star* building, you are made to feel that your presence as a pedestrian is barely tolerated.

Captain John had no particular opinion pro or con about the Gardiner. However, *Regeneration: Toronto's Waterfront and the Sustainable City* (1992), the final report of the Royal Commission on the Future of the Toronto Waterfront, echoed Fulford's sentiments. In it, the Commissioner, David Crombie, states,

> The combination of the elevated portion of the Gardiner Expressway, Lake Shore Boulevard underneath it, and the rail corridor beside it has created a physical, visual, and psychological barrier to the Central Waterfront. It is a constant source of noise and air pollution, a hostile, dirty environment for thousands of people who walk under it daily, and a barrier to thousands of others who risk life and limb to get across or around it. The Gardener Expressway is not only a road; it is a structure. As it processes traffic, it stunts land use; meant to move us along, it limits our opportunities.

He further notes that highrise waterfront development "added to the growing sense that the public was being cut off from the lake and that the shoreline, rather than being used as a park for people, was becoming a housing tract."

In *Emerald City*, however, the architectural critic John Bentley Mays does not "sympathize with the claim, very often heard from its critics, that the Gardiner is somehow impeding our access to the lakefront, like the former Berlin Wall, an insuperable obstacle between landlocked Torontonians and a realm of forbidden delights we can now only dare dreams about, or see on television." He asked what the Gardiner blocking access to, and concluded, "Nothing. You can drive or walk or take the light-rapid-transit car under it or over it at many points."

You could, but it was a decidedly unpleasant experience. As for the Gardiner, what was to be done with the damn thing? Many futuristic proposals were made, but none realized. Oddly, the Gardiner was no longer nearly so important a mass-transportation route. By 2006, the TTC buses, streetcars, and subway lines carried 47 per cent of inbound commuters, non-Gardiner auto routes 26 per cent, and the province-run GO Transit, begun in the 1960s to take lakeshore commuters downtown, 19 per cent. The Gardiner? Eight per cent.

The cover of a pamphlet-like Lunch and Dinner Menu for "Captain John's Harbour Boat and Banquet Facility," showed the Captain in his trademark arm-banded navy blazer, white trousers and shoes, invitingly holding open a port-holed door. The menu took note of his neighbours. The CN Tower, whose pointy top suggested from a distance that it might have been more aptly named the CN Hyperdermic, opened in 1976, and was at the time the world's highest freestanding structure. Nearby was the Metro Toronto Convention Centre, opened in 1984, and the SkyDome in 1989, later banally renamed the Rogers Centre, home to the Toronto

Blue Jays, winner of the 1992 and 1993 World Series. Also nearby was the Air Canada Centre, Bay Street home of the Toronto Raptors basketball team and the Toronto Maple Leafs hockey team. The latter had been transplanted from their legendary Gardens on Carlton Street.

Highrise cheek by jowl to Captain John's was the Westin Harbour Castle, which the real-estate high-riser Robert Campeau had built just to the west in 1975 (along with two apartment blocks) as the Harbour Castle Hotel. Campeau, whose Toronto developments included the Scotia Tower, the city's second tallest skyscraper, had overreached himself in the 1980s when he acquired two U.S. department-store chains, one the owner of Bloomingdale's: the debt bankrupted his corporation. Dating from the 1980s a few blocks further were the glassy Queen's Quay building; federally funded in the 1970s, Harbourfront Centre with art galleries, theatres, and marina; and, as Fulford notes, "more boring apartment buildings than anyone cared to contemplate." Nearer at hand, and much more recently, construction on condominiums started in the parking lot next to Captain John's *Jadran*, as development crept inexorably eastward toward the Portlands. This, of course, was part of the condominiumania that had seized Toronto. If there was a big hole in the ground, a tall condominium building was sure to fill it.

As Gene Desfor, Lucian Vesalon, and Jennifer Laidley note in "Establishing the Toronto Harbour Commission" in *Reshaping Toronto's Waterfront* (2011), that by the late 1960s the urban shoreline held only remnants of its industrial and cargo-handling past, and the choice seemed to lie between high-income condominiums and waterfront access plus affordable housing. Of course, all bets would have been off had Toronto won one of its Olympics bids.

The Greater Toronto Area now held 5.5-million people. The prevailing development mantras had become "mixed-use," "sustainability" and, given the size of government deficits, "public-private partnerships." It was no longer expressways, and all that they entailed. To the Captain, the Gardiner Expressway hadn't made much difference one way or the other to his floating enterprise. He did recall that in the 1970s a developer had offered to demolish the Gardiner free in return for the land while traffic followed a tunnel under Lake Shore Boulevard. Nor had the opening of Harbourfront Centre, the Queen's Quay Terminal, or the Harbour Castle Hilton greatly increased his volume of customers – though in the 1970s and 1980s he'd had the benefit of spillover from events the Harbour Castle couldn't handle. Nor had it made much difference in 1999 when the Toronto Harbour Commission became the Toronto Port Authority.

The Captain thought the Spadina Expressway should have proceeded; it would have brought more traffic to the waterfront and environs at a time when the SkyDome and the CN Tower hadn't existed: the more objectionable portions of it could have burrowed underground. On the other hand, he generally liked the ideas found in *Regeneration: Toronto's Waterfront and the Sustainable City,* the nature-loving report of the Royal Commission on the Future of the Toronto Waterfront. In 1967, a waterfront Plan for Metropolitan proposed lakefilling, chains of artificial islands, open public spaces, and marinas. Forty-four years later, the mayor's brother, Councillor Doug Ford, proposed a megamall and colossal Ferris wheel on the Port Lands, 450 industrially polluted hectares at the mouth of the Don River. In the end, control of development was left to Waterfront Toronto, a three-government agency created 30 years earlier. Waterfront Toronto had envisaged a new mouth created for the Don

River to replace its current stagnant channel, a riverside park, and a community blending housing and commerce. In the Captain's view, the multiple reports, plans, and studies of Waterfront Toronto had only yielded decades of dithering and a billion dollars of costs – some of it paid by his own over-the-top taxes.

The Captain's sometimes inconsistent opinions had one common thread: anything that would bring people to the waterfront was good, especially in winter, when the bitter cold was intensified by gusts blowing off the lake, or from the highrise canyons up the hill. Toronto's development model should emulate San Francisco's, the Captain thought. Admittedly, San Francisco had milder weather. He would also have liked the city spruced up a bit, and panhandlers deterred from assailing his customers on Captain John's Pier.

In recent decades, cities with frontage on oceans, rivers, and lakes, all over North America, Europe, and Asia had begun to turn their attention away from suburban sprawl to exploiting waterfronts whether in the form of colossal developments or modest boardwalks. In the Introduction to *Reshaping Toronto's Waterfront*, Gene Desfor and Jennifer Laidley had listed changes on Toronto's 40-mile Lake Ontario shoreline.

> Particularly over the past hundred years, 'things' have been constantly changing: new landforms have been produced; a river has been straightened; shipping and shipbuilding facilities expanded and contracted; manufacturing plants established and demolished; water mains and sewers laid; grain silos built and razed; housing torn down and condominiums constructed; streets built and rebuilt; commercial

> and office buildings have sprouted; city beaches appear and disappear; parks and gardens come and go; cultural and entertainment venues are fabricated; an airport [on Toronto Island]; and more.

This list does indeed suggest that on the waterfront a great deal had transpired on, though such extensive changes were surely inevitable, given that they had been going on over the course of more than a century. Although some might have taken pride in what had been accomplished on the waterfront, there remained for many a nagging sense that the city had failed to properly exploit its natural advantages.

After 1999, civic pride had taken a glancing blow when Yonge Street was deposed as the longest street in the world in the *Guinness Book of World Records*, which now called the Pan-American Highway the world's longest "motorable road." Gordon Lightfoot's lyrics for "On Yonge Street," on his album *A Painter Passing Through* (1998) claimed:

> Everywhere you go in a city by a lake
> Back there in the flow you may give a hand a shake
> Everyone you pass seems to want to say hello
> Even late at night on the freshly fallen snow

Lightfoot's lyrics about Torontonians' fellow feeling were a shade implausible, especially at the bleak windswept corner of One Yonge Street and Queen's Quay West. But there was one touch of humanity there in the person of Captain John, the good host. The Captain had most of the virtues, and a few of the vices, of the independent self-made business person, but he could not be mistaken for the average Kiwanis or Rotary joiner and booster. The ships he had berthed on Queen's Quay West had added character to a characterless street. If the *Jadran* stuck out like a sore thumb, it was because the span of waterfront on which they floated lacked a thumb of any kind. A privately owned, quietly rusting anachronism, the Captain's ship wasn't glossy. It wasn't slick. It wasn't trendy. It wasn't the product of overdetermined design. Unwittingly, he had set himself at defiance against the *folie de grandeur* of Montreal's Mayor, Jean Drapeau, who had done his best to wreck his city's unique architectural blend of French provincial Catholic and Scottish baronial, and saddled it with the crippling debt incurred in construction of the Olympic Stadium (the "Big O," or the "Big Owe.") The Captain had embarrassed the grandiose, geometrically minded urban planners around him by setting down an emblem of the quaint and quirky.

A DAY ON THE WATER

It's early November. Today the Captain is limping more than usual. He has been having a problem with his leg; a specialist suspects that a hip is responsible and might have to be replaced. He's dismayed that he has to wait two months to get an MRI. "Imagine you're an immigrant just off the ship and you go to a doctor and are told you have to wait two months," he says. But still, like the rest of his family except for his sister Angela, only a few months old when she died many years earlier, and another sister, Kristina, a tailor of men's clothing when she died of an undiagnosed liver complaint in 2008, he has a remarkable constitution. Perhaps the limp is the aftereffect of the powerful radiation treatment for the cancer that had almost taken his life as a teenage refugee in Austria. He wears a built-up shoe and arch supports. There is no ambient music aboard the *Jadran*, which of course adds to its appeal. At any rate, it is hard enough for the Captain to hear as it is, since the radiation took away half the hearing in his right ear.

Late in August he had gone to St. Michael's Cathedral, where Cardinal Alojzij Ambrožič was lying in state. Ambrožič, a farmer's son, had born not far from the Captain's Slovenian birthplace and, a 15-year-old, he had fled to Austria and refugee camps in 1945, before coming to Canada three years later. Reserved, privately kind, sometimes blunt, he had been a New Testament scholar. Named Cardinal by John Paul II, he was, so the *Globe and Mail* obituary said, "an unmistakable and unshakable theological traditionalist who opposed gay marriage, the teaching of sex education in Catholic schools and the ordination of women." He and the Captain had met several times, and once he had come to the ship. Looking down at the Cardinal's hands wrapped in a rosary, the Captain had touched his ring. It made him think of how, on his mother's eightieth birthday, he had given her a ring with the birthstones of her children and said, "This ring will go with you to the grave so you're never alone. You will have every one of us with you." He didn't know whether the Cardinal's ring went into the grave with him.

But the Captain is not brooding on mortality today. He has never been one to brood; in any case, today he will be too busy. The Royal Winter Fair is on at the Canadian National Exhibition grounds, and he has been getting good business from the more affluent farmers, who order martinis and manhattans instead of the wine or low-margin mineral water his customers usually do. In fact, business has been good so far in 2011, especially for brunch, and his customers have been undeterred by the fact that the operator who leases the jammed adjacent parking lot charges a flat rate of $30.

Business could take the form of three busloads of French tourists booked through a Quebec tour agency, with whom he has dealt since the mid-1990s. They arrive in Montreal and then travel to Quebec City, the

Thousand Islands, Toronto, Niagara Falls, and Ottawa. They have to be in and out of Captain John's in one and a half hours. Or it could take the form of 20 local Vietnamese sitting down to dine on lobsters ferried in on trays. Or it could be a "Caribana Heatwave Party" with a DJ and a bar, a yearly event since the mid-1990s, for which as much as a thousand people line up from the street to the gangplank at 11 p.m., some of them from Jamaica and Trinidad, and all of them ready to party until 5 a.m. The weekend before Halloween, he'd hosted 400 diners, requiring him to hire extra staff. Often he thanks the guests as they leave, sometimes presenting the ladies with a dusky rose.

Business this year is good. By contrast, the previous year's receipts had been dismal. Companies had cut back on receptions and Christmas parties. Back in the 1970s it had been agreeably different: the Captain could bill event bookers for unlimited drinks; there had been no such a thing as a cash bar. In the past, he had worked with the convention bureau to promote Toronto on tours in U.S. cities, but there was no money forthcoming for it now.

He breakfasts big, as he always does, and no later than 8 a.m.: cereal, fruit, eggs twice a week, smoked salmon, herring in sour cream. When there isn't a blizzard, he breakfasts on the open deck, a good time, taking in the view and tossing crusts to the gulls wheeling above their inland sea, purposeful yet free of care. Unlike the gulls, the Captain usually skips lunch, relying instead on a teabag in a glass of hot water. He will eat something late at night. The rest of the day he is on his feet. "I work all day like a machine," he says with some pride.

After breakfast, he returns phone calls. Then he may get into his 1996 black Cadillac Fleetwood waiting in the adjacent parking lot: the vanity license plate says

CPTJ; a 1977 mate of it gathers dust in a garage. He will drive off to shop for dry or canned goods at a cash-and-carry. He gets his oysters, Malpeques from Prince Edward Island, delivered fresh. He schedules weekly specials, depending on price and what's available. Salmon's his most popular fish, along with the seafood platter. His brunches will include eggs, ham, sausages, cold meat and fish items, a marrow-rich dish called pork osso bucco, rice, vegetables, seafood chowder and onion soup, cold shrimp, salads, and a sweet table.

After he gets back, dozens of small tasks await him. On the phone he gets a $350 price on a used dishwasher. A serviceman had come the previous day to fix the old dishwasher: he didn't have a replacement switch, but charged him $75. Another serviceman came: another $75. That dishwasher has caused problems before. In 2008, the city's Public Health Department had fined him for several offences, including "Operator fail to maintain premises free of sewage back-up." The sewer connection was three floors below: a young inspector had mistaken water and a white dishwashing chemical for sewage. The Captain chose to pay the fine on the other charges rather than fight them.

Whenever it's within the scope of his abilities, he does plumbing, welding, carpentry, and wiring himself, crediting his handyman knowledge to the way he was brought up. He sweeps the front hall and gangplank: a lot of dust has been coming in from the condominium construction site beyond the parking lot. Inside, on a table below a ship's wheel, are bulletins from St. Michael's Cathedral.

He passes by the long interior wall with their photographs of distinguished police officers and visiting celebrities. One of the former Lieutenant Governor, Pauline McGibbon, and the former Yugoslav Ambassador. One of the stout Councillor, Joseph Piccininni, being fed by statuesque blondes. One of Captain John Mann, his shipmate aboard the *Jadran*'s transatlantic crossing, who later became Toronto Harbour Master. There's a photo of the Captain and three men, one in a gorilla suit – possibly a memento of Barbary apes during the *Jadran*'s refuelling stop in Gibraltar.

Here, too, are framed thank-you letters from churches and community associations, and a certificate from the Canadian Forces Liaison Council having to do with a 2006 trip with police officers and firefighters to Executrek Esquimalt on Vancouver Island, an event to promote enlistment in the navy reserves – during a day at sea the Captain had watched a "man overboard" demonstration. By the washroom door is a certificate from Red Carpet Canada: "John Letnik completed Course in Profitable Restaurant Merchandising." In his quarters, he sometimes adds to a box of memorabilia: colour photos of himself in white cap, maple-leaf tie, crested blazer with gold-braided cuffs, white trousers, the outfit he wears on special occasions – Boris Spremo's pictures.

Some days he may have visitors, not all of them welcome. A large nondescript fellow wearing a cap wanders in. The Captain asks if he can be of service. The man says he's "looking at the restaurant." The Captain, who finds him "kind of funny looking," curtly tells him, "We're not open." He exits, and the Captain goes out to make sure he's left the boat. A suited pair from the Royal Bank of Canada deposit business cards and brochures with him. "It's strange to see bank people looking for business," he remarks. "These days they don't even let you walk in the door." So much is done on the Internet now. For at least the past 50 years, the Captain laments, small business was responsible for the banks' growth – "We're the ones who made them" – but now the banks sought bigger prey.

Aboard the boat, it's not all a one-man show. Depending on requirements, he employs a full-time cook, a kitchen helper, a dishwasher cleaner, a receptionist, variable numbers of part-time help, and four servers. Before he retired for health reasons, one of his workers, a Portuguese named Alberto Figuera, had waited on tables for 41 years. Fong Wong, a Chinese, has been the Captain's cook for about 20 years. A Spaniard with a neatly edged moustache named Luis Cordero has been working here for about 16 years, though the Captain hasn't kept track, nor the number of years clocked by a Serbian named Boris Filipovic.

Among his employees, the Captain is constantly on the move. Maybe that's what keeps him slim. He likes to tell the media, "I'm not rich. I didn't have a rich uncle. Work is my hobby, business, and profession." Prep for dinner begins no later than 4 p.m. — the Captain can be found in the kitchen, slicing a giant slab of ham, or he may be boiling salmon bones, ideal stock for his seafood chowder. He opens his door to the public at 5 p.m., closes at 10 Monday to Friday; Saturday and Sunday brunches start at noon, priced at a modest $12.95. He used to charge more when they included lobster and crab.

Whether it's in the main dining room, the Dubrovnik room for banquets, or the two cozy, richly decorated rooms the Captain uses for small weddings and the like, he seldom has trouble with violence or drunkenness on the part of his customers, though in the early years, there had been a lot more drinking, and the Captain sometimes had to take away a customer's car keys and drive him home. But in more than 40 years he could count on the fingers of both hands the number of times he had to call the police.

But it's a tough trade, running a restaurant. He says, "I have no friends in the restaurant business any more. They gave up or they died."

♦ ♦ ♦

Today, early November 2011, the Toronto waterfront weather is no more dismal than on any other November day. A stone's throw across the bay from Captain John's seafood restaurant gloomily stands a fringe of leafless trees: the Toronto Islands are not looking their best. Nor is the *Jadran*: the D in the *Jadran*'s name is missing, causing it to be a gap-toothed *JA RAN*. On cold windy overcast days even the white gulls and piebald ducks on the dark water look discouraged.

The author of this book, notebook in shoulder bag, is turning off Queen's Quay West to ask the Captain another long series of tedious disconnected or repetitive questions. Once, while leaving after a previous interview, he had fumbled with his shoulder bag. The Captain had called out, "Don't drop it in the harbour. I don't know how to swim."

"But you're the captain."

"Sailors don't know how to swim."

Confronting the sidewalk is a flaked weather-beaten wooden effigy of the Captain ("Best Seafood in Toronto") and a big red-and-black painted anchor supporting an even larger sign advertising the restaurant. To the left is a rope-framed restaurant menu; another notes, "Capt. John is offering Domestic Beer or Glass of Wine for $3.75." A wall of a small structure that vaguely resembles an ice-fishing shack announces, "Welcome Aboard." A crude fresco depicts the Captain: some joker has sketched in a Salvador Dali moustache.

The *Jadran* looms alongside Captain John's Pier. The vessel rides medium-low at the moment; after pelting rain it will rise. When the water level is at its lowest, the gangplank will get so steep that customers may feel in need of mountaineering equipment. Across the slip are plastic flowers in wicker baskets, replaced in season by small bright clumps of annuals; a tub with two usually live, now dead evergreens; miscellaneous ironmongery and kettle-like pots.

Shipside, more evergreens and outsize menus; a framed cover of a Slovene magazine circa 1997; a plywood board depicting ocean-view Frenchman's Cove, Newfoundland; a blurred Toronto skyline complete with CN Tower; intriguing facts about lobsters; a map of the Gulf of St. Lawrence area including a region called "Gaspecy"; white creatures swimming in a blue sea; and a view of a port, on whose hilltop is a peddler with a pack of wooden articles – actually, based on a postcard, a lake near the Captain's hometown of Lenart, Slovenia.

Further on, embedded in cement, lie chains like those lugged by Jacob Marley in *A Christmas Carol,* and a huge bronze-painted propeller salvaged from the *Normac*. There is a wooden cutout of a badly drawn Captain John, whose swollen hand uncertainly grasps a lobster, next to him a torso in sailor uniform with an empty oval where tourists to stick their faces in for photographs. Then the frayed red-carpeted gangplank, at the top a Lions International logo sign (the Lions hold their annual meetings aboard) and, hung from the ship, a life preserver.

The Captain materializes at the top of the gangplank by the brass lamps fixed to sides of a black door with oval glass inserts. He spots the visitor. With a self-mocking grin, all put-on nautical pomposity, he cheerfully calls out,

"Permission to enter the ship!"

ACKNOWLEDGMENTS

The first debt I must acknowledge is to John Letnik, who endured the many hours of my questions with patience and forbearance. This book could not exist without his powers of memory.

Several readers scanned the text for errors of fact and interpretation. Alison Sutherland, who comes from an old Toronto family and knows the city in ways I cannot, reviewed the manuscript and employed an eagle editorial eye. The Ljubljana poet, translator, and broadcaster, Marjan Strojan, read with a view to Slovenian matters. Concerning local, provincial, and national history and politics, John Pepall, author of *Against Reform*, brought to bear an encyclopedic knowledge of Toronto society. They are responsible for improvements to the book, not for any remaining flaws. I am grateful to them all.

To the useful print and online sources such as blogs and websites that are mentioned in the text I also count such books as Mike Filey's *Toronto Sun* columns on Toronto history, often gathered in volumes with the series title *Toronto Sketches* (1995-2004) as well as his *Toronto: The Way We Were* (2008), Misha Glenny's *The Fall of Yugoslavia: The Third Balkan War* (1992), Mark Mazower's *Hitler's Empire: How the Nazis Ruled Europe* (2008), and Jasper Ridley's *Tito: A Biography* (1994) provided useful historical background. Two Toronto memoirs offered valuable context in different ways: James Chatto's *The Man Who Ate Toronto: Memoirs of a Restaurant Lover* (1998) and Tony O'Donoghue's *Front Row Centre: A Perspective on Life, Politics and the Environment* (2001).

No serious research can be undertaken without recourse to public libraries and archives. For their assistance, I thank the staff of the Toronto Reference Library and the City of Toronto Archives, as well as the staff of the Federal Court of Canada's Toronto office.